The Culture Wars Within

An Examination of Marriage in the Context of Culture Conflict

Editors

Azubike Aliche

Stella Nwokeji

Contributors

Brown Ogwuma

Rev. (Dr.) Sunday Eke-Okoro

Evelyn Nwigwe

Valentine Iwuchukwu

Chime Okafor

The editors dedicate this book to their spouses, Stella Nkechi Aliche, RN and Emmanuel Igweze Nwokeji, M.D., for their patience and support during the researching, writing, and production of this book. Without your encouragement, care, and sacrifice, this book would not have been completed in the short time that we worked on it.

Limit of Liability/Disclaimer of Warranty: As the publishers and authors of this book, we made every effort to check the accuracy of the information contained in this book. We also applied our knowledge of the Igbo culture, as well as insights from our professional trainings. However, we make no representations or warranties regarding the accurateness and completeness of the contents of the book. Each marriage is different, just as each person in couple relationships is unique. We expect that readers will view the advice and strategies suggested in this book, for a successful marriage, as intended to be used with caution and to be adapted to suite their individual circumstances. Nothing in this book is designed to replace the services of a qualified counselor or mental health professional.

To obtain a copy of this book, please contact Azubike Aliche at: zubbiks@alichechildcenter-ngr.org or call 856-906-6167.

The Culture Wars Within

TABLE OF CONTENTS:

Acknowledgements

Since 2005, at least 15 Nigerian men have killed their wives in the United States! Some of the killers are Igbo men!!

Anthonia Eberechi Iheme of Hennepin Minnesota and Melvina Ojukwu of Garland Texas had a few things in common: They were both Igbo immigrants and registered nurses. But, more importantly, they were killed by their husbands! Until her death in 2008, Mrs. Iheme had two children, a four-year-old boy and a three-year-old girl for Michael Collins Iheme who shot her to death. Mrs. Ojukwu was 36 years old when Theophilus, her husband, used a hammer to bludgeon her to death while she slept, on March 25, 2007. Other Igbo wife killers and their victims include:

- Chidiebere Omenihu Ochulor, felled by husband Kelechi Charles Ochulor on New Year's Day 2008, in a Maryland suburb of Washington DC.

- Roseline Unachukwu, 34, of Los Angeles, whose body was, reportedly, tied to a truck and dragged around the streets, by her husband.

- Gloria Uchechi Anya Onwuka, 42, of Tulsa Oklahoma, killed by husband John Onwuka, 49, on August 19, 2006.

Interestingly, all the affected woman had been nurses. It is, also, important to note that the cases cited in this article are those reported in the mass media, which suggests that the crisis in our marriages may be greater than is known, as many lesser forms of domestic violence go unreported. Alarmed by this development, Chief Newman Nwachukwu decided that something had to be done to draw attention to this ugly phenomenon. He came up with the idea of writing a book that addresses intimate partner violence among the Igbo in the Diaspora, and passed that idea to me. He also collated the reports of these tragic acts of intimate partner violence. So, I owe to Chief Nwachukwu the original idea of this book project and I remain grateful to him for his foresight and for giving me the opportunity to lead this project. The idea was to come up with a book that will help "To Save Igbo Marriages in the Diaspora," and that became my rallying cry.

Once I had accepted the challenge of exploring the state of Igbo marriages in the Diaspora, I knew that I needed help to do it, successfully, hence I sent out word for help. I knew that I needed to collaborate with other Igbo intellectuals and community leaders. I knew that I needed additional intelligence on what happens behind the closed doors in Igbo homes. The goal was to discover what Igbo couples expect of their mates, given the realities of the conflict between their cultural heritage, regarding gender roles, and what is prevalent in the US and other parts of the Western world. More importantly, we needed to find out what works, from the perspective of people who have made a success of their own relationships. In this regard, I am eternally grateful to Dr. Stella Nwokeji who enthusiastically embraced the idea and ended up as a co-editor of this publication. I am also thankful to Dr. James Chukwuma Agazie who bought the idea of a book such as this and even offered to co-author it. Dr. Agazie, an author himself, gave me a copy of his own work on marriage. I'm also grateful to Dr. Amanda Uzor, another early enthusiast of the idea of the book and who worked with me in the early stages of the book project. In this category, also includes Adolphus M. Ohaya, to whom I am also indebted. I cannot thank the contributors to this book enough, particularly Mr. Brown Ogwuma who drew up the survey instrument used in data gathering and who was deeply involved in major decision making on key issues for much of the period that this book was being conceived and developed. Other contributors deserving of my gratitude are Dr. Sunday T. Eke-Okoro, Lolo Evelyn Nwigwe and Mr. Valentine Iwuchukwu. I am also grateful to Dr. Obinna Ubani-Ebere for his encouragement and initial promise to contribute a chapter to the book.

In the course of recruiting partners for this project and bouncing the idea off individuals and groups of Igbo people, the electronic groups on the Internet were used. In the process, more people than I may have recorded names contributed in enriching the stock of ideas and perspectives that influenced the content of this book, one way or the other. I am grateful to all those people who spoke to me on the phone or wrote comments regarding the book project. Here, I will acknowledge only a few of these individuals, the ones whose names I was able to capture. They include Onyinye C. Onyekwere-Onyagoro, MD; Joy E. Chidi, Obiefule Uwadineke, Albert Nguidjol, Hyacinth Ezeamii, Reuelson Tough, Chukwuemeka Onyesoh, O.J. Igwe and someone who identified himself as Oke Osisi. A few others, including Ms. Joy Nwanganga, Felix Obioha and Mark Onyenemezu also made invaluable contributions to our work, for which I'm grateful. I'm also indebted to Odengalasi Uzoma Nwaekpe, Esq., for accepting to review this book before it is presented to the public. Okezie Amalaha of Atlanta also deserves credit for all the materials that he forwarded to me for reference, as I worked on the book.

Finally, on December 30, 2011 the Igbo Marriage Book Project organized a focus group teleconference, to seek to find out what works for happy couples. Twelve people called in and I'm grateful to each one of them, including Ephraim Udo Jacob, Okechukwu Onyeizu, Mr. Ogalaonye, Mrs. Uju Nwobodo and Chief Nwadike. Each of you spoke with passion and your insights helped enrich our work. Also, because of the sensitive nature of this subject matter, there are a number of people who talked to us under a promise of anonymity and that the confidentiality of their information will be maintained. We remain grateful to them, particularly because your input made it possible for us to complete our work, without compromising the quality of the book.

Dr. Nwokeji and I acknowledge, publicly, the sacrifices made by our spouses and children, as we spent countless hours working on this book. We thank them for their patience and understanding.

Azubike Aliche

AZUBIKE I. ALICHE, M.Sc., MSW, LCSW

Mr. Aliche is a licensed Clinical Social Worker in the State of New Jersey. He graduated from the Rutgers University School of Social Work in 2007 with MSW degree. Before that, Aliche completed undergraduate and graduate studies in sociology and mass communication, respectively, at the University of Lagos, Akoka, Nigeria. In the 2010/2011 academic year, Aliche completed a postmaster's certificate program in couple and family therapy (CFT) at Drexel University in Philadelphia, PA. In October 2008, he joined the services of the University Correctional Healthcare service of the University of Medicine and Dentistry of New Jersey (UMDNJ), as a mental health clinician, where he provides psychotherapy to parolees of the New Jersey State Parole Board in the southern New Jersey area. He also works, part time, providing intensive in-home psychotherapy to children and adolescents with behavioral issues and their families. He maintains a small private practice in Vineland, New Jersey where he works with couples and families on relationship problems and their mental health needs.

Before coming to live in New Jersey, Aliche distinguished himself in the practice of journalism in Nigeria. For nine years, he worked in some of Nigeria's best newspaper houses, including its flagship The Guardian Newspaper (Lagos) where he started his career in 1989, and the Sunray Group of Newspapers (Port Harcourt) where he rose to the position of editorial page editor in 1997. A prolific writer and public affairs commentator, Aliche's articles appeared in the Philadelphia Inquirer in 1998-1999. Aliche is a recipient of the "Best Journalist in the Rivers State of Nigeria, 1996" and of the Goldsmith Research Award of the Joan Shorestein Center for the Press, Politics and Public Policy, JFK School of Government, Harvard University, for 1997. He's the author of many books, including Tales from Africa (2002) and Udo: The Peace of a Blind Father (2009).

Originally from Abia State, Nigeria, Aliche is married to Stella Nkechi Aliche, a nurse, and the couple has children. He can be reached through zubbiks@alichechildcenter-ngr.org.

STELLA E. NWOKEJI, MSN, NP-C, Ph.D, JD

A native of Imo-State, Dr. Stella E. Nwokeji is married to Dr. Emmanuel I. Nwokeji. They are blessed with four wonderful children, Briana Chiamaka, Brittany Ijeoma, Brian Igweze, and Brandon Chukwuka. Dr. Nwokeji received her baccalaureate and master's degrees in science from the Union University, Germantown, Tennessee, and University of Memphis, Tennessee respectively and a PhD in nursing from The University of Tennessee Health Science Center in Memphis, Tennessee. Dr. Nwokeji, recently, obtained a Juris Doctor (JD) degree and plans to use her law training for the advancement and empowerment of Nigerian women.

Dr. Nwokeji holds a variety of clinical and research positions working primarily in Internal Medicine facility as a Family Nurse Practitioner and a research investigator. She is the Executive Director of Total Care Medical Services, Memphis, TN. In addition, Dr. Nwokeji volunteers as a family nurse practitioner at a local community clinic in Memphis, TN where she has been recognized yearly as a primary care provider providing quality healthcare to those in need. Dr. Nwokeji is actively involved in the Nigeria community in the Diaspora and enjoys reading, dancing, traveling with her family. She can be reached at enwokejiob@yahoo.com.

Brown Ogwuma, LCSW

Mr. Ogwuma is a Licensed Clinical Social Worker who has worked in the human services field for over twenty years. In addition to a master's degree in Social Work and a clinical licensure, he holds a bachelor's degree in Accounting and an MBA and is the author of two books: *Playing God* and *Root that Binds*. An avid community organizer, Ogwuma resides with his wife in Peekskill, New York.

Rev. (Dr.) Sunday Theophilus Eke-Okoro

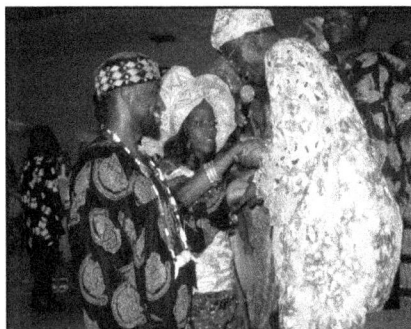

- *Eke-Okoro (right), blesses daughter's marriage, at Igbo traditional marriage ceremony*

Dr. Eke-Okoro is the Senior Pastor, Jesus Is Lord Baptist Church, Sicklerville, New Jersey. He holds the Dr. Med. Sc. degree of the University Linkoping, Sweden 1985. Dr. Eke-Okoro holds the M.Sc. degree from the Simon Fraser University, Canada 1979, as well as M.Div. degree from Palmer Theological Seminary, Philadelphia, USA 2002. He obtained the B.Sc. degree from the University of Ibadan, Nigeria 1976.

Until he relocated to the United States, Eke-Okoro was Associate Professor & Chairman Department of Medical Rehabilitation, College of Medicine, University of Nigeria 1986-1996. Upon coming to the United States, he worked as a Research Fellow at the University of Medicine & Dentistry of New Jersey, Stratford NJ. 1996 – 2000.

Dr. Eke-Okoro is a Member, Executive Board, Baptist Convention Pennsylvania & South Jersey. Prior to that he was Coordinator, Evangelical Fellowship in the Anglican Communion, Saint Andrew's Anglican Church, Enugu Nigeria 1990 -1996, as well as Zonal Chairman/Zonal Representative, Abakpa Zone, Scripture Union, Enugu, Nigeria 1993 -1996.

Also, Eke-Okoro is an Elected Member, New York Academy of Sciences 1994, and was Visiting Research Fellow, Department of Clinical Neurology, Oxford University, England 1989.

Eke-Okoro has published 24 scientific articles and 13 religious publications. He counsels couples and maintains a blog on Marriage and Family Enrichment. His core belief is that "Marriage is not a bed of roses." "You need to work on it to make it succeed"

Eke-Okoro is married with five children (2 boys and 3 girls).

Evelyn Nwigwe, MSW, ACSW

Lolo Evelyn Nwigwe was born in Onitsha, Anambra State of Nigeria. She was raised in Ekwulobia. She later married Chief Sam Nwigwe from Umuchu in Aguata Local Government Area of Anambra State of Nigeria.

Lolo Nwigwe is a social worker with Alameda County Social Services Agency in California. One of her current supervisors describes her as a very compassionate and effective social worker that has helped so many youth reach permanency. She works with teenagers in the foster care system that are preparing for emancipation. Lolo Nwigwe also shared that she has always been a social worker most of her life. She has an extensive history of helping others, volunteering and teaching. For example, while still very young, she taught women in the village, who could not read or write how to read and write Igbo language without charge. She was helping disadvantaged individuals achieve a higher quality of life back then in the village. For some years, Lolo Nwigwe has volunteered with Medical Mission groups to Nigeria.

Lolo Nwigwe now lives in the United States of America with her husband. They have four children.

Valentine Chukwudi Iwuchukwu

Mr. Iwuchukwu was born in Ozubulu, Ekwusigo Local Government Area of Anambra State on the 14th day of February, 1966. His academic training was in civil law. Val Iwuchukwu is the Head and Principal Partner at Eastern Empire & Co; a Legal & Property Consultancy firm in Lagos and Abuja, Nigeria. Val is the author of BLUEPRINT ON SECURITY AND STRATEGY FOR ANAMBRA STATE GOVERNMENT (2009). He also brought his literary talent to bear when he wrote NIGERIA PORT REFORM: A TREATISE ON PORT DECONGESTION, in 2010. Val is regarded in many circles as a natural philosopher and a perfect gentleman. He lives in Lagos Nigeria with wife and children.

Preface

In the course of gathering materials for writing this book, we talked to a number of people who live in problematic marriages. As it turned out, the very first interviewee's story was typical of what happens when a marital relationship operates under the influence of two cultures – the host (American) culture and the heritage (Igbo) culture. Although this woman blames the failure of her marriage, essentially, on the interference by her sister-in-law, it quickly became apparent, as she told her story that other cultural factors, particularly gender roles and expectations, were at play. This woman had passed up an opportunity to proceed for further study at the University of Nigeria Nsukka and married right after secondary school, following pressures from family members and relatives on both sides of her family. As is usually the case, her husband was the first to leave for the United States. It took 10 years before she could join him. And when she did she waited another four years and raised two children before her husband could agree that she can go to school in the US. After it became clear that her husband wanted her to, practically, be full time housewife, with little or no education, she made a move, on her own, to go to school. And this was the source of a major crack in their relationship, which eventually led to separation and divorce. If this couple lived all their lives in Nigeria, there is a good chance that this marriage would be subsisting today, even with the same circumstance described above. If you listen to this woman's story, in full, it becomes clearer why Igbo marriages in the Diaspora either labor under great strain or eventually snap and break apart. A focus on the conflict of cultures that is at the root of many struggling Igbo marriages is what this book is all about.

What we find is that partners in a typical Igbo marriage in the Diaspora become indifferent and unloving due to a lack of insight on how each is reacting and adjusting to the pull and push of conflicting cultures – the host culture and the native culture. Igbo people in the Diaspora need to learn, in practical and specific terms, how their lives and marriages are being shaped by the forces of culture. If they do, marriage shouldn't be such a struggle for many of us. So, this book explores the different ways in which Igbo men and women are responding to the conflicts in cultures, as reflected in their relationships. At the end of the day, reading this book will help Igbo couples improve their communication with each other, as they become more aware of the issues underlying difficult and painful marriage. It is designed to help Igbo couples enrich their relationships and, ultimately, save their marriages.

Although love remains the single most important factor in a lasting relationship, a deeper understanding and insight into the cultural factors that impinge on marriage is needed to reduce frustration and disappointments and pull many Igbo marriages in the Diaspora away from the precipice. After the storm there should be room for peace and quietness. This book is aimed at helping Igbo couples who are struggling with their marriages to fall in love again. The book aims to change relationships after gaining understanding of the obstacle that cultural forces exert on the wheels of stable marriages. Instead of heading to divorce courts, to the detriment of our children, Igbo couples should be able to share the rest of their lives together. The book aims to help people discover who they are and what shapes their lives, so that they can understand each other and stay married.

This book makes every effort to avoid the usual attitude, among the Igbo, of blaming women for any marriage failure and the associated mistrust and resentment towards them. On the other hand, it also does not treat women as victims, as is usually the case in many American circles. The book is fair to both sexes, as it is based on an objective and balanced analysis of facts, as obtained from interviews and other secondary sources. The goal is to assist Igbo couples build relationships, based on dignity, mutual trust, personal responsibility, cooperation and love. It is aimed at breaking down barriers, which conflict of cultures creates in relationships. Tension is palpable in many an Igbo marriage and this book offers strategies, from different perspectives, aimed at reducing tension and increasing happiness and intimacy in relationships. This is done by raising awareness of the place of conflicting cultures in our lives and the harm that this does to our marriages. The cost of tensions, frustrations and disappointments in marriages can be very high, not only in attorney fees but on our mental and physical health, which the Igbo cannot afford. As the media reports quoted elsewhere show, many lives have been lost already to domestic violence.

For sure, many Igbo couples start out their marriages in love. However, what we see, often, is that the passion gradually disappears, soon after an Igbo woman joins her husband in the USA, particularly as she becomes increasingly aware of the ways of life of the host country, including the opportunities and protections that the laws, structures and institutions of the American society has for women. Part of this is seeing, firsthand, the patterns of relationship among American couples, which is often envied and emulated without much thought to the fact of inherent culture conflict that is bound to arise when Igbo couples embrace American patterns of relationship.

For one thing, many an American marriage often falters and as much as 50% break up, despite that they operate under a relatively homogenous cultural setting. If this is the case, it can only be imagined how things can quickly get complicated when a couple is walking a tight rope between two dramatically opposite and contradictory cultures, which is the case with many Igbo couples. Igbo couples deserve love in their marriages and families but, to achieve this, they need to pay attention to how their host society and the new culture is becoming a barrier to love, fulfillment and satisfaction in their marriages. The book offers practical guide on how to respond to these societal forces, in a way that is productive, rewarding and functional. Knowledge of the new society, in relation to the society of origin, will create understanding and moderate expectations of one partner about the other. Right now, for example, there are still Igbo men who expect their wives who work full time and yet meet the expectations of the traditional Igbo gender roles for women. On the other hand, there are Igbo women who would rather be the boss at home if they earn more than their husbands, with inherent conflict following the

11

attendant reversal of traditional roles. These are just a few examples of sources of conflict in some Igbo marriages that reflect a culture conflict. Understanding that culture is dynamic, role reversals possible and that conflict is inevitable may be of help and that is part of the focus of this book. It is the basis for the practical techniques for creating loving relationships and solving marital problems that this book provides.

The problems that culture conflict creates in our marriages will always be there. The challenge before Igbo couples is whether to allow these to create resentment and rejection in their relationships or present them an with opportunity to deepen intimacy and increase trust, caring and love. This book is designed to help them meet that challenge. It does this by providing Igbo couples the awareness and tools to deal with the effects of culture conflict in their lives and marriages, in a manner that, eventually, promotes understanding, love, support and intimacy. This book forces any Igbo person in a relationship in America to dig deeper into the self and society and see what you need to change or live with in order to create more love and passion in your relationship; to walk that fine line in negotiating a balance in the often conflicting demands of the American and Igbo cultures.

A few points are worth making about the book, before signing off on this preface. One is that, while culture conflict remains the dominant paradigm in the book, it is important to state that other lesser perspectives are used in seeking an understanding of conflicts in many an Igbo marriage in the Diaspora. As is reflected in the questionnaire used in the surveys, socio-economic and mental health issues were considered factors at play. In particular, the poor help seeking behavior, particularly in mental health issues, among the Igbo in the Diaspora may be masking the level of mental health problems that trigger the occasional violent behaviors that characterize many of the conflicts among Igbo marriage partners. Also, as this book attempts to provide insights into why a marriage that works well in Igbo land is beset with many problems, once it is transplanted in American soil, the limits of the book should be realized. It is not a book of therapy but one that fosters understanding and knowledge. So, reading this book does not preclude Igbo couples experiencing trouble in their marriages from seeking the services of marital or couple therapists and other relationship experts for the transformation that they can get from working with a good therapist or counselor. Anything that Igbo couples do to increase the love in their lives, fulfillment in their relationships and the stability of their marriages will be worth the investment, if only for the welfare of Igbo children in the Diaspora who, in large numbers, have problems with identity and cultural dissonance. To all who read this book, our wish is that you end up with insights and tools to make your marriage and other intimate relationships happier and keep divorce at bay.

Azubike Aliche

June 2012

Chapter 1

Our Culture, Our Heritage

by Azubike Aliche

The Igbo society is patriarchal! It is male-dominated! This is reflected in all facets of life but more so in the relationship of the husband and wife. There are just a few personal examples to illustrate this. My late mother called my father "Master." Never did I hear her call my dad *Chiehika*, his name. Also, during the *Biafra-Nigeria* War, we ate just about anything to survive Nigeria's blockade of the secessionist enclave that was the former Eastern Region of Nigeria (*Biafra*). Among these was a beautiful bird called "Ovo" in local dialect. My mother, like any other woman in my part of Igbo land, was barred by our tradition from eating "Ovo" meat. In fact, when it comes to meat, the choicest parts were reserved for my father – the gizzard, the heart, liver, etc. Patriarchy also meant, in most parts of Igbo land, that descent is traced from the father's side of the family (patrilineal descent, as opposed to matrilineal). The consequence of that is that boys are pre-ferred over girls.

In my part of Igbo land, there is a saying that: "*ahubeghi egbe na anya, asi na nwanyi erighi ya*! *Egbe* or kite. Many times, it's seen flying in high altitude and hardly perching. So, few hunters that I know have brought it home for dinner. But, on the rare occasions when they did, women were forbidden from eating this elu-sive bird. Also, the cola nut holds a special place in Igbo culture. The Igbo do not grow it in large quantities but they eat it more than the growers. They don't just eat it; they use it to celebrate. Presenting cola nut to a visitor is a sure statement that the visitor is received with open arms. No public event of the Igbo is com-plete, unless kola nut has been broken and shared. Yet, while all the rituals that accompany the presentation and breaking of cola nuts go on, women are only spectators. No woman, no matter how old or accomplished, ever gets presented with kola nuts, unless it is time to eat it. This is one more reminder that men, no matter their age, are considered superior to men in Igbo culture.

In fact, women in traditional Igbo culture were barely regarded as members of their family of origin. They, for all practical purposes, were regarded as belong-ing to their families of marriage. If a woman marries, she takes on her husband's family name. She changes her religious denomination or affiliation. I have seen Igbo women turn Muslim, as soon as they married a Muslim. Not long ago, I at-tend a wedding ceremony here in the United States where the chairman of the reception party kept emphasizing what he enunciated as the "No Return" policy of the Igbo, regarding marriage. That, in a nutshell, says that a woman does not return to her family of origin, under any circumstance, once she marries. A more charitable interpretation of that is that divorce is not acceptable in Igbo culture. Of course, if the woman dares return, she can't inherit any part of the family property, often reserved for male offspring. The problem with this is that it gives a message to men that they can treat their women however they like, since they have no other place to go.

The Bride Price
It's more than Bride Price; it's Cash and Carry

The whole concept of bride price is often confused with dowry, by outsiders. The bride price is central to the traditional marriage process in Igbo land. In fact, it is at the heart of the process. It is what confers legitimacy to marriage, not the marriage certificate. Unlike in dowry, the suitor pays the bride price and, often, he pays steeply. Negotiations for the actual bride price and other things associated with the traditional marriage can last for hours, sometimes days. This may be unintended but paying the bride price tends to give the man a sense of entitlement, to lord it over the woman. It makes him tend to treat his wife as part of his property. It subordinates the woman to her husband. It makes her possessions and earnings that of her husband. If she fails to submit to her husband's authority, she could be physically assaulted and few people will raise an eye brow, including her own family, in some cases. In many cases, the power that the payment of bride price confers on a man lasts a life time. It gives him the right to control his wife. It gives him a right to be unaccountable to his wife and to get away with such things as adultery which sometimes makes the woman to live perpetually in fear and awe in her matrimonial home, as she can be thrown out any time, should she demand a fair treatment from her husband. Depending on who a woman marries, she could lose her dignity and sense of self. That situation hasn't changed, totally, even now when working women are able to contribute money towards their own traditional marriage.

Bride price has been blamed, often, for the late marriage among Igbo young men and women, in relation to other ethnic groups that have no place for bride price in their marriage process. In traditional Igbo society, a young man did not have to earn enough money on his own to marry; parents often stepped in to pay the bride price for their sons. Over time, as girls got higher education, the bride price went up, many times beyond the reach of young men. And, as Western education and culture intruded, young men spent less time in the farms with their parents and more in the classrooms, a situation that meant that, for many years, they could not earn money to marry on time. Meanwhile, the new values made arranged marriages unpopular. Part of the reasons that parents married for their sons was to increase the farm hands and to reward the sons for their help in the farms. The bright side of the current situation in which men mature and marry by themselves is that they tend to treat their spouses better, reflecting that many of these women are also educated and mature.

Traditional Marriage

"As a father of five beautiful girls, I realized that, someday, the wedding bells will ring, ringing my pocket dry! So, I decided to stage all the weddings the same day ..." I couldn't stop laughing until my ribs began to crack the first time I heard this advert message from a well known insurance company. More than the fun it

brings, the ad reminded me that I'm in America, not Igbo land. In traditional Igbo society, no man bothered about spending money on his daughter's wedding. Of course, there were hardly any weddings, just traditional marriage. At a traditional marriage ceremony, prospective suitors would pay for everything done, in addition to the bride price. The only obligation that a family had to their marrying daughter was to buy a box of clothes and cooking utensils that she needs to set up her kitchen when she goes to her husband's family. Even today, a suitor pays for his wedding, if he wants one with his bride. It's not the business of the bride's family.

Until Christianity became a dominant religion in Igbo land, and the colonial government introduced formal marriage laws, no one needed to wed in the church or register marriage in a court. The traditional marriage was sufficient for all purposes. Even now that both court marriage and church wedding are common, traditional marriage remains preeminent. No self-respecting father or couple would go for any other form of marriage, without starting with traditional marriage. Traditional marriage is believed to confer the most blessing on a union of man and woman, as the libations to ancestors are a part of, if not the soul of the marriage. In many cases, church and court marriages are done to fulfill legal requirements or official purposes. In the traditional marriage, all family members and the entire community are witnesses to the marriage and their presence confers legitimacy to the marriage in a way that no other form of marriage does.

It's in the Mail

Once upon a time, Igbo young men and women didn't need to meet, date, fall in love, etc, before marrying. Their parents took care of arranging their marriage. In some parts of Igbo land, a baby can be marked for marriage to another baby and the two just wait until they are of age to consummate the relationship. That was before the introduction of Western culture in Igbo land, through education and Christianity. As more and more young people began to "drink of the White man's wisdom," they realized that they have a right to choose their own girlfriends and life partners. Problem arises when some of these young people have to leave their culture and country to travel abroad to further their education, particularly in the United States. Yet, they still preferred girls bred in their own way, the Igbo way! What to do: marry and mail them their wives! That is the genesis of the "mail order" wives syndrome!

Igbos in the Diaspora who had their wives "shipped" to them had to rely on the judgment of their parents and, sometimes, siblings for the selection of their wives to be. Some had friends or siblings recommend wives for them. In some cases, only pictures were exchanged before the traditional marriage is conducted, in their absence. In the days before the mobile telephones became available in Nigeria, some couples married without even speaking on phone. With thousands of miles separating Igbo land and the United States, it made economic sense to save travel money and have one's family take care of arranging a wife for their son. Besides, some of the sons did not have proper documents to travel into and out of the United States. So, it became convenient to use money that would otherwise go into international travel to invest in traditional marriage, by proxy. The only problem was that the arrangement didn't always produce two individuals who were compatible in many fundamental ways! In some cases, the goals for the people involved were not the same. For example, the man may have needed a companion in his wife while the wife may have needed a ticket to make money for self and family in the United States.

A Man's World!

Those of us who are educated and have lived in America for many years can take a look at the Igbo society and declare confidently that it's a man's world. But it hasn't always been so crystal clear. Even some of our former classmates who have lived all their lives in Igbo land may not see it, so clearly. For them, it's just natural that women have to serve men or do the chores. Aren't we all raised that way? I mean, as kids, were we boys ever asked to go wash the dishes when the girls were there? If money was scarce, were we not the ones sent to school, leaving our sisters at home, even when they were more intelligent? Were boys not home when our sisters and mothers took the hoes to the farm to weed the grass? Did anyone worry much where we were, playing, as boys? I mean if you think of it now, there were always things that you can remember that indicated that boys were treated differently from girls. Don't get me wrong, the Igbo protected their daughters! As boys, we took the heat and fought the predators that had their eyes on our sisters. But, if you look at it critically that "protection" amounted to paternalism. If we wanted to treat the girls as equals, we would have discovered that they did not need us to fight for them. But it all looked natural to treat them as "weaker vessels." But that's where the treatment of women as inferior to men started: in our homes and from the cradle! It all looked natural. At least, that's what the Igbo culture told us – it was our way of life and everyone appeared comfortable with that, until we brought our wives here or had them mailed to us!

For many of us, when our wives joined us here, we expected them to, in the words of Ekaette, the former deputy editor of *Sunray Saturday Special* newspaper, play both wife and mother. In practical terms, we wanted them to cook, clean, raise our children and serve our romantic needs. One problem, in the United States, is that, in many cases, they work too and sometimes make more money than we do. More importantly, they are joining us in a society that accords women their full rights, as human beings, not as women. Although America also has a history of mistreating women, it has weaned itself of those laws and practices that held women down so men can ascend. Today, the US has all kinds of laws and enforcement mechanisms that ensure that women can assert their rights to dignity and respect. In America, it's no longer a man's world!

Where is the Respect Mrs. Wife?

Igbo men almost always demand respect from their wives. I suspect that this sense of entitlement comes from paying the bride price. The only other reason I can think of is that Igbo men are generally older than their wives, in many cases by more than 10 years. In Igbo culture, age is revered. And people generally demand respect from others younger than they are. In the traditional Igbo society, men were also generally the bread winners. That status, often, give them a sense of superiority over women (particularly their wives). Women were not just expected to respect their husbands; they were required to respect their in-laws, particularly anyone in the extended family older than their husbands. As part of the code for respect, a woman is expected to call anyone older than her husband in the family by a name or appellation that acknowledges that they are older and deserving of respect. Names such as "Dede (men)" or "Da (women)" are used in some parts of Igbo land. Even today, only few women will call their husband's older relatives by their first names.

When I reflect on my own childhood, I recall that girls have always had a stricter code of conduct, reflecting the fact that they were being groomed for marriage. I can think of things that we, as boys, did freely but girls were barred from doing. We could sit however we wanted; we could climb, we could speak loudly, pose as masquerades, etc., without being reminded that we were girls who one day would be married to a man. Even table manners were different for girls, who were often reminded that certain habits cannot be taken to a future husband's house. So, the message was always there, no matter how subtle, that the girl needed to behave well to fit into a new household when she's of age. And part of the reason behind this was that the girl's behavior in her husband's home always reflected back on the training that she received in her own mother's kitchen. So, families took steps to avoid any possible shame that could come their way in the future if they failed to do a good job of bring up their girls. And good girls got rewarded by being married in the neighboring villages. Bad girls were likened to a hen with fractured legs. In Igbo parlance, the fractured hen represents a bad product. The conventional wisdom was that you cannot sell such fowl near the home. So, bad girls, if they ever found suitors, were destined to be married away from home where they suffer isolation and remain at the mercy of their husbands and their family members. At a time when marriages were largely arranged and only followed elaborate background check of the bride and her family, good behavior, particularly respect for elders earned the most mark for girls and made a difference as to whether they remained on the shelf for a long time or for life. Even if a disrespectful girl gets married, she faces greater odds of being a target of domestic violence than a girl who respects her husband and his family. In some cases, younger girls in the husband's family are sent to beat up women who do not show respect for their husbands and their family members.

The good news, from my own experience, is that girls are not usually treated as inferior by their own siblings or boy peers. I don't remember knowing anybody who disrespected his sister because she's a girl. In fact, older sisters exercised the same authority over younger siblings, no matter their gender. Even in primary and post-primary school I also did not notice boys disrespecting their female class-mates, simply because they were girls. There's no question that roles were gender-based, whether at home or school but these were understood in terms of differ-ences, rather than from a superiority-inferiority paradigm. At home, for example, boys were generally exempted from household chores. Much of their own work was outdoors and in the farms. In the same way, while boys will cut the grasses, girls would either weed or knit. Yet, I can't recollect any indication that boys felt entitled to respect from girls, without earning it. Even when they married, women had the respect of men and everyone in the family, as long they did not challenge the authority of their husbands. This authority comes in part because of a belief among the Igbo that the man is the head of the household. Even outside the fam-ily, married women were widely respected; that respect deriving from their status as married and from fear of hostile reaction from their husbands should anyone disrespects them. And just like it has for men, the Igbo traditional society had a number of titles reserved for women achievers. Of course, an unmarried woman hardly gets respect in Igbo land of the old, no matter how wealthy she becomes. In my part of Igbo land, such a woman who remains in "*Okpulo* (family home)" is often ridiculed by the luckier married women of her family.

And when it came to wealth, married women never really had wealth inde-pendently. In those days, irrespective of how much income that a woman con-tributed to the family purse, she remained "ori aku" (someone who consumes the wealth of her husband). In other words, a woman's income belonged to her husband. The situation has not changed much even now many married women answer "*Odozi Aku*," (one who safeguards the family wealth), instead of *"ori aku."* *There is a saying in my own part of Igbo land that "oke nwanyi mgba tara, ya ezi di ya."* This, literally, means that a woman is obligated to account to her husband any money she makes from dancing. Here, dancing can mean another word for a business venture, sale of certain products, to mention but a few. In reality, it applies to all income by a woman, irrespective of how it is generated. Again, it looks to me that the golden rule is that when he pays the bride price a man buys the rights to any money that his wife makes, subsequently. There were minor ex-ceptions, though. For example, women generally retained any money made from selling palm kernels, after the palm nuts have been processed for palm oil and the husband has taken delivery of the palm oil. Even then, any money realized from cracking and selling the palm kernels go to buying food stuff for the fam-ily. If a woman needed clothes, it was expected that her husband will provide these for her. Also, in many families, women didn't have to account for proceeds from cocoa yam and cassava from their farms. But they were also expected to use them to take care of the needs of the kitchen, where they were expected to be in charge. In fact, any woman who was poor at managing the kitchen, and thereby her husband's stomach risked being thrown out and sent back to her family of origin. That is why part of the socialization of young women emphasized the attainment of culinary skills and sensitivity to the needs of a man. Hence, the saying the gateway to a man's heart is his stomach.

Sex – Behind Closed Doors!

Indeed, sex in the traditional society happened behind closed doors, and for the most part, in the dark (night). Men and women spent much of the day outdoors, in the farm, essentially. Besides, children were protected from anything sexual, apparently in effort not to corrupt their impressionable minds. Usually, a man would have his own bedroom and his wife (wives) joins him in his bedroom for sex. In polygamous households, wives took turns to sleep with their husband. In many cases, a woman cooked for her husband on the day that it is her turn to sleep with her husband. Even when, as was the case later, a man shares the same room/bed with his children, efforts are made to postpone sex until the children are seen to be deep asleep.

Up until the early 1970s, women were expected to arrive at their husbands' households as virgins. And many communities, reportedly, had ways for the husband to test this, including using a white bed sheet on the first night of sex to check that blood stains followed what is supposed to be the first sexual experience. It's hard to know if any girl ever failed this test and what the punishment was. It appears to be more of a social control measure to encourage abstinence from sex before marriage, something that was considered the norm. Related to this, at least in my own part of Igbo land, is a practice that allowed the bride's family to get more money from their prospective in-laws. In those days, a woman will run back to her family of origin, as soon as the new husband spends a night with her. When this happened the husband goes with money and palm wine to give to her parents before she returned to her matrimonial home. These days, the money is paid in advance, as part of the bride price. In my part of Igbo land it is called *"ego igbala ta oso."* Literally translated, it means money paid to avoid the bride running back to her family upon her first sexual encounter with her husband. It has to be noted that sex was generally reserved for the night.

The whole idea of requiring girls to retain their virginity until marriage reflects another evidence that girls were treated differently from boys. Although premarital sex was basically a taboo in Igbo land, for boys it was enforced more in the breach. The definition of a good girl, fit for marriage, included that she does not sleep around with men! The perception was that premarital sex damaged a girl, including her image in the community. In fact, it was hard for such a girl to find someone to marry her, even when the sex was as a result of rape. That is why young girls cultivated chastity and ensured that they were seen to be self-controlling and keeping a distance from boys. If a girl was perceived to be promiscuous it reflected on her upbringing. That's why the entire extended family and even the entire family invested efforts in monitoring and counseling the girls, as to acceptable sexual behavior. And out of wedlock pregnancy was an anathema. Any product of that pregnancy was called a "bastard" and generally stigmatized, if not discriminated against. In fact, female circumcision was promoted as a measure to limit sexual stimulaltion and therefore promote responsible sexual behavior.

Again, because sex happened behind closed doors, it's hard to determine how much sex dominated the life of Igbo couples in the traditional society. But it does seem that polygamous men got more sex, if they wanted. From the little experiences and anecdotes that I can piece together from my early years, I imagine that sex was one instrument of bargain available to women but this was more effective in monogamous marriages. For instance, it appears to me that a woman who hasn't got much clothes and other goodies from her husband could withhold sex until the husband bought those needed items. At times, this became the source of domestic disputes but it appears that many women were able to hold their grounds until the husband played ball. However, in polygamous relationships, the social arrangement and manipulating room available to the man of the house, allowed the man to get sex as needed. He could rely on his special wife *(Nwanyi nma)* to make up for any shortage from any protesting spouse. The reader is to note that the concept of a special wife *(nwanyi nma)* and what it is called can vary from one part of Igbo land to another. In most polygamous homes, a man almost always had a wife that he treated special and kept close to his heart. She could fill in his needs even when others are not available. On the whole, it appears to me that men generally respected a woman's right to consent before any sexual encounter. I recall how Dede Ugonnaya, an uncle, used to boast that he never would have sex with a sleeping woman. Translated, this means that a real man will get a woman's consent first before sex. Given what I know, I won't be surprised if that consent is coerced, sometimes. Dede Ugonnaya also used to say *"Onye iwe ajughi otu,"* meaning that a man is never too upset to decline an opportunity to have sex. What I read from this is that sex was usually an instrument for reconciliation between couples when they quarreled. On the whole, it's hard to say how much sex was used for recreation or whether it was ever used in the context of a relationship, the way we understand it today, in America.

Chapter 2

Problem Marriage Not Igbo Thing

by: Azubike Aliche

A few people have asked me to justify the writing of this book. They ask me what is special about the problems, if any, that Igbo marriages go through in the Diaspora. My attitude has always been to acknowledge that the statistics, where they exist, about domestic violence or other symptoms of a troubled marriage, are not worse for Igbo couples. Estimates are that one quarter of all marriages experience violence, irrespective of the cultural background of those involved or their social and economic status. I've also added, though, that the trend towards breakup in Igbo marriages is troubling and need to be arrested. Igbo couples need to begin to be aware of and address issues that may make Igbo marriages lose their unique stability.

As far back as the 1980s, statistics from the Federal Bureau of Investigations (FBI) had shown that 50% of women killed were murdered by their current or former partners. I don't know if this is true for a majority of Igbo women who are murdered in the Diaspora. Also, figures from the Centers for Disease Control, show that about 50% of marriages contracted in the United States will crumble by their 10th anniversary. Igbo marriages in the Diaspora are yet to attain this speed of dissolution. But that does not mean that there is no need to be concerned about the health of Igbo marriages in the Diaspora.

The "Rule of the Thumb"

It is instructive that there was a time in the United States, for example, when it was legal and culturally accepted for a man to "beat his wife with a stick," as long as it is not bigger than his thumb and the beating is not on a weekend or after 10.00 pm. This was the source of the "Rule of Thumb." In fact, a state like New Jersey did not have a domestic violence law until 1982. Ironically, at that time, the rate of divorce was negligible in the United States. The time of low divorce rate in the United States coincided with a time when women did not have the right to vote – a right they gained in 1922 – and Congress was dominated by men. Well, since then, there has been the Woman Suffrage and the Civil Rights movement, among other revolutionary events and movements that changed the fortunes of women forever. And with freedom and equal rights come sharp increase in tension in marriages and upward trend for divorces.

Igbo Marriages Shouldn't Have Problems!

Given that most Igbo couples share core cultural values, it's a wonder that there is so much tension and, in some cases, domestic violence fatalities in Igbo marriages in the Diaspora. Almost always, Igbo men in the Diaspora will go home to marry a wife or have one mailed to them from their own part of Igbo land (preferably). This is not usually for romantic reasons, for many of us who came here as bachelors know that Igbo girls can't beat American girls in anything romantic, including sex. In return for a woman that shares the same cultural values with them, Igbo men make such sacrifice as flying 5000 miles to the East of Nigeria to pay bride price for a woman, spend hundreds of dollars in immigration filing fees and wait endlessly for the immigration formalities to be complete before taking possession of their priced jewel. When they marry an American woman, for example, they make sure to call her a name that differentiates her from an original Igbo woman. They know that when they marry someone that does not share their core values, they may be faced with a choice to force the wife to adopt their own values or live with culture conflict. Either way, the risk for marital conflict is high.

Of course, one of such shared values is the concept of a "good wife." A good Igbo wife does not abandon her husband, even when he's abusive. If she does, she loses the support of her family and community. She risks being ostracized, if she leaves! Under the traditional Igbo gender structures that place men above women, a good wife looks the other way when her husband brings in his concubine. In fact, some women were made to cook and serve their husband's girlfriends in their own homes! It is important to disclose here that, at the time when this was the case, the man was almost always the bread winner, or owned the primary sources of income in the family, usually landed property, farmlands or cattle. It is also important to note that, in that era of Igbo history and culture, marital conflicts were resolved within the traditional family structure or the native court system, which was also controlled by men who made the rules.

Why they have problems!

In North America and Europe, the laws and social structures are different from what they are in Igbo land. They are protective of women. They do not permit vertical control of women by their husbands, as is the case in Igbo land. Here, in the United States, women are accorded equal status with men and any attempt to control them as non-equals creates tension. Vertical control is, relatively, tension-free, if it is from a parent to a child but not husband to wife. Besides, many Igbo women are primary income earners or strong secondary income earners in their households. Our women now demand, like their American or European counterparts, to be controlled horizontally by their husbands if at all. They demand to be treated as equals. Can Igbo men handle that without seeking to take a page from their fathers' play books?

There may be other reasons why domestic violence may be a part of many Igbo marriages in the Diaspora. When researchers look into the problematic issues for men who have been implicated in domestic violence, they find evidence of high stress, few relational skills, mental health problems, substance abuse history, poor communication skills and control issues, among others. For women who are involved in domestic violence, researchers find evidence that they struggle with such issues as past history of physical, sexual and emotional abuse, mental health issues, substance abuse, poor communication skills and dysfunctional family system.

Stress! What is that?

For Igbo men and women living in the developed countries of the world, stress can come from childcare (on average we have more kids than Americans or Europeans), household chores (particularly for the women who have to work and, in some cases, do all the chores in the house), growing debts, interference from in-laws and other relatives, parenting challenges when it 's hard to find house-girls, sexual problems with partners, few opportunities for advancement because we have accent, trouble with boss or co-workers and more. And when stress overwhelm us you find that many of us suffer endemic headaches, sleeping problems, fatigue, constipation, high blood pressure, change in appetite and more, sometimes without knowing where they are coming from. Even when we find that it is stress-related, many Igbo men or women will rather brush it aside and soldier on as if the body does not need maintenance, just as the big cars that we drive. Do we make time to engage in stress management measures that we need? As we chase the dollar or pound, for instance, do we make time to get enough sleep? Do we take a vacation with our families, as often as needed? Do we get enough physical exercise at the gym or outdoor activities? Do we have hobbies? Do we make time for such mundane things as listening to music? Do we take time to treat ourselves to good lunch or dinner outside the home either alone or with our families once in a while or even as a matter of routine? More importantly, do we make time to see a health professional before things get out of hand?

I'm not sure how many Igbo men, in particular, who would take to drinking, smoking or substance abuse in efforts to deal with stress. But a lot of people in America and Europe do. And they end up creating more problems than they had, originally. For example, those who use alcohol to deal with stress may end up with depression and then more stress, as alcohol is a depressant that slows down the central nervous system. Even tobacco, which first acts as a stimulant, eventually ends up acting as depressant and tranquilizer, as it contains nicotine. Besides, people who smoke are at risk to develop life threatening diseases, such as lung cancer and heart disease. These conditions, in turn, cause stress for the rest of the family, due to the considerable amount of time and money needed to treat and care for those afflicted. Even the grief and loss associated with any death resulting from cancer or heart disease can be a source of stress for a long time. Many years ago, when I was growing up, living and working in Nigeria, I used to think that cancer was a white man's disease and that all chronic diseases in Igbo land was caused by the enemy, through witchcraft, but the reality today is that I know better. Igbos also suffer from cancer and in some cases, it is preventable if we watch our lifestyles and make some lifestyle modifications that are needed for our good health.

Relational Skills, Communication Skills – What are they?

Have you taken time to reflect on how you relate to your spouse? I mean what regard you have for him or her and how you express that regard. Have you checked how you speak with your partner – your choice of words, your tone and inflection of voice, as you speak, etc? These matter, if you plan to live in peace and for a long time together! I know many Igbo men who say it's un-African to regard your wife as an equal partner. *Tufiakwa* (don't even mention it), they would say, and remind you to consider that they are the man of the house, the head of the household! People like to point to the fact that they paid the bride price and brought the woman here. And they ask you, what their gains are from all that investment in money and time? They remind you that, by Igbo tradition, the man of the house is entitled to the submission and obedience of his wife, or she can leave. After all, they say, they can marry another woman the next day. They remind you that Igbo women in America are lucky and that they should count their blessings because they have more social and economic opportunities than their counterparts living in Nigeria. They point to what could have been their fortune or lack of it, if they had married someone residing in Igbo land. They also remind you that, in Igbo land, they could be sharing their husbands with other legitimate wives, as polygamy is still alive and well in Igbo land! Wow! These may be plausible arguments but do they guarantee the stability of their marriages?

However, the reality on the ground is that the North American and European environment, where we live, requires a different set of attitudes and skills to live in peace with one's intimate partner. For whatever it is worth, Igbo women in the Diaspora live and work with their hosts and they like to be treated with respect and dignity. Igbo women married and living abroad are saying in many different ways that they are listening to their American and European counterparts and getting new interpretations of the traditional practices that they had hitherto taken for granted. They like to be called "Honey" sometimes, maybe more frequently than we realize, and not just *Ogbodiya!* Our women are saying, in many different ways, that they don't want to be talked down on, and in public. They are asking that certain family matters be treated with confidentiality, not discussed at beer parlors or Igbo parties, often held every weekend in the summer to celebrate one thing or the other. They are asking to be consulted when major family decisions are being made, and not just at implementation stage, particularly when it involves projects and issues for which the money they earned is to be used. They are asking to know about what the man is planning to do before he discusses it with his parents and or siblings.

Who wants to see the psychiatrist?

In our native Nigeria and many other African countries, mental health is not accorded the attention that it deserves. In fact, many African governments have no departments in charge of developing and providing mental health policies, programs and services. Where they have, these departments are underfunded and understaffed. Because of the social stigma attached to mental health disorders, sufferers are often stigmatized and abandoned by family and friends. Where they are not abandoned to roam the streets, they are confined and secluded in the home, to avoid the shame it can bring to the family. Among Africans, including the Igbo, there is widespread belief that mental health conditions are afflictions from evil spirits and no one wants to be associated with it in any form. Many Igbo immigrants in the United States subscribe to this attitude or view. Back home, in Igbo land, we have a culture in which mental health problems are denied and kept a secret until they can no longer be concealed.

That this attitude negatively affects our willingness to seek help when struck by a mental disorder is plausible. It is quite possible that our family belief systems – what we learned or believed about mental illness from our families of origin - is

27

holding us back from seeking help for mental health issues and that this is playing a role in increasing domestic disputes among Igbo couples in the Diaspora. Media reports show that, since 2005, at least, 15 Nigerian men have killed their wives in the United States. It is entirely possible that these men had mental health issues that were never addressed, leading to their use of violence to settle domestic disputes. With all the hassles associated with living in a foreign land, it is possible that our people can suffer from common mental health problems, such as depression. Even, those of us who served in the Biafran Army during the civil war may still be dealing with post-traumatic stress disorder. Also, living with domestic violence can be traumatic for both men and women such that those involved need the services of qualified mental health professionals.

Little Things that Mattered

In the traditional Igbo society, much of the means of production were vested in the man, the husband! I mean land; economic trees, such as the palm trees, cocoa, etc; cattle and other economic animals such as dogs, goats, sheep, etc. Even the rivers that were collectively owned had rules that allowed men to fish and exploit other aquatic resources, to the exclusion of women. Related to that is that boys, not girls, were offered formal education at the advent of the European missionaries who brought schools to the area. The widely accepted view was that the place of the girl was in the kitchen. Even the churches did not ordain women as priests or put them in other positions of authority. Instead women were offered inferior, supporting roles. Even in the farms where women toiled all day for much of the farming season, yam, the king of crops, belonged to the man.

One consequence of this lopsided distribution of economic resources in favor of men is that men became the expected and, in fact, actual bread winners in the household. And women become dependent on men for basic needs. There was no doubt that, by tradition, the man was the head of the household. It appears that the logic was to make the man an effective head of the household, not a figure head, by strengthening his capacity to control the family. And many men used their social position and wealth to manipulate and cajole their wives to get what they wanted. They used it to play stick and carrot. In the process, they used this status not just to provide intimate apparels for their wives, when they are happy with the wives, but make them to stand out in the community of other women! It was clearly the role of the man of the house to buy clothes for his wife, particularly loin clothes or "wrapper." For most Igbo men, the unwritten rule was to use this power to buy wrapper for their wives, to get the woman to do their bidding or deny them the choice clothes, when they are not happy in the relationship. It was used to secure obedience, loyalty and conjugal rights, in some cases.

It is no wonder that a husband's power to buy his wife wrapper became one of the tools of control that he had over his wife or wives, and a powerful one at that. This was even more important in polygamous families. Here, there was always a favorite wife, normally known as *nwanyi nma*. The favorite wife can always be spotted from a distance by her outstanding dressing. Many times, this favorite wife is the youngest of the wives in a family. At other times, *nwanyi nma* secures that status by virtue of her ability to keep the love of her husband above the other wives by virtue of her loyalty, beauty, culinary skills or sheer people skills. No matter how the favorite wife acquires and maintains her status, she can count on having many full boxes of clothes and jewelry at any particular time, courtesy of an adoring and giving husband! Because of this, *nwanyi nma* is usually the subject of envy from other women, within and without the household. For this, her husband would often take steps to protect her.

In a sense, from what I knew growing up in the village, there appears to be an unwritten social contract that the man would provide wrapper (clothes) for his wife or wives. The women expected that and would withhold certain services, including sex, from a husband who is not buying them clothes. This used to be a source of tension in some marriages that was never spoken about, publicly. On the other hand, a man's worth was often measured by how his wife looked in public. So, the expectation was that a man who had money will use it to make his wife look good in public. That expectation limited the extent to which a man would use the buying of wrapper to extract service from his wife without appearing indigent. It is important to mention that, in those days, almost everything that a married woman wore was made from the wrapper, including the blouse and, sometimes, the head tie. At that time, a man didn't need his wife to be present before he could buy her clothes. The man's choice of clothes was, invariably, accepted by his wife. In any case, many women at the time didn't have much of their own independent self image. Their identities were tied to those of their husbands'. In fact, most women were not called their own given names. They were portrayed as appendages of their husbands. For example, my mother was more often called Chiehika's wife (*Nwunye Chiehika*) than Nkechi, her name from her family of origin or even Grace, the name that my dad gave to her. A woman's stock of names was not complete until she marries. Everyone from her husband to mother-in-law, father-in-law or any other close family member reserved the right to give her a name.

It is noteworthy that giving a newly married woman a name was not an empty ritual. It was an opportunity for the man and his family to express the state of their minds, particularly their emotions following this fundamental rite of passage in their lives. If you read carefully into the meaning of the names, you can find something about the family history, desires, hopes and aspiration at that point in time. Since the bride and groom never would have the opportunity of a courtship or friendship before marriage, many of the names reflected the groom's expectation from the relationship. Names like Obidiya (groom's heart/choice), *Omasiridiya* (the groom's favorite), *nwannadiya* or *nwannediya* (groom's sister) expressed a sense of love and closeness that the groom envisages, as much as it is of the likeness that the groom has of the bride. I use the word likeness instead of love, given that love could not have developed in the short time that partners usually knew each other before marriage and in a society in which some form of arranged marriage was the order of the day. There were also names like Ogbodiya which suggested that the groom expected a more equitable relationship with his wife, as ogbo can be interpreted to mean friend or mate, someone of equal status. If a mother-in-law liked what she saw in her new daughter-in-law, she gives her names such as *Nwanyinweulo* (the woman who owns the household), Adanma or Adam (my daughter or beautiful daughter), etc. Of course, every married woman has an extra name: *oriaku* (beneficiary of her husband's wealth). On their part, every married woman reserved the right to give her husband a name or what she plans to call him. With this, you find that women, invariably, chose names that reflected the man's authority over them. My mother, for example, called my father "Master" all through their married lives. She never called my dad Chiehika, as this could be interpreted to mean disrespect. Some called their husbands *Dede* (the older one). Rarely did you find any woman who called her husband by his name, as this was considered disrespectful even by the women themselves. Part of the reason that wives were expected to respect their husbands was that the husbands were almost always older than their wives and age was revered as a matter of tradition.

The Road from the Stomach

If woman wanted to retain the affection and favor of her husband, one sure way to achieve this was to be a good cook. The general belief was that the shortest route to a man's heart passed through his stomach. This belief would have originated from an era when little intellectual work took place; a time when the farm was the mainstay of the economy. At that time brawn, not brain was needed and food was needed to fuel the body for the work at the farm. In that circumstance, it is understandable why the woman with the best culinary skill will have a soft spot in her husband's heart, since the men did the heavy lifting at the farms. It is no wonder that mothers started early enough to teach their female children the fundamentals of good cooking and housekeeping. A good, well trained woman always would make special delicacies for her husband, for that added advantage. Common food stuff, including beef and melon were often prepared in special ways, for example *akpuruakpu mgbam*(melon) or *Ngwongwo* (beef or cow skin), to make it more appealing to the man. Even special spices are used, particularly if the man likes them, to bring out that special taste that he likes. In fact, the competition for the man's heart, through his stomach is more intense in polygamous families, where the contest, wittingly or unwittingly, is for the favorite wife, *nwanyinma*.

A good wife was also expected to have food ready for even the unexpected visitor. In my part of Igbo land, women would prove their worth as housewives by their ability to feed any visitor to the house with well cooked food and in the right amount. Women took pride in doing this. They wouldn't let anyone visit and leave with empty stomach. Indeed, the wife was seen as the head of the department of kitchen and a good wife took steps to show that they are in charge, and effectively too, by the way they feed not just their husbands but their visitors. This is more so on major market days or local festivals, when people stop over unannounced. In any case, it was not the custom to call ahead and give a host notice that a visitor or relative would be coming. So, most women, even the poor ones, would have food ready most of the time or be in a position to get food ready in a matter of minutes to few hours.

Chapter 3

Matrimonial and Domestic Violence Laws of Nigeria

by: Valentine Iwuchukwu

In Nigeria, Marriage remains a voluntary union of a man and a woman. This means that, in Nigeria of today, before a union could be termed a valid marriage, it must be established that there is a man and a woman involved, to the exclusion of all others.

Marriage, when contracted is universally accepted anywhere in the world. To ensure this universal acceptance, laws guiding the institution of marriage are made in such a manner that they must pass the litmus test of crossing international boundaries. This is so because foreign nationals resident in another country have the right to enter into valid marriage in the country of their residence if they so wish. Laws, as accepted and legitimate standard of behavior, shape the life and practices of those in a particular region or country in which such laws are enforced. What is lawful in one country may be a crime in another and this applies to laws that concern matrimonial causes. Due to the influence of religion, pressure groups, culture and tradition, matrimonial laws differ not only from one country to another but from one ethnic group to another. It also can differ from one community of the same ethnic group to another. Laws guiding matrimonial causes are therefore multifold, complex, flexible and dynamic but nevertheless effective.

In Lagos State of Nigeria, for example, the State House of Assembly in March, 2012 passed into law a bill that no longer criminalizes bigamy. Previously, it was a crime for any person male or female to marry another spouse when the previous marriage is still subsisting. However, the new law does not free the offender from liability in torts, which entitles the victim to approach the court for damages over the breach of contract of marriage. In other Southern States of Nigeria, any person convicted of bigamy ends up in jail for up to 2 years, in addition to the Court declaring the subsequent marriage a nullity.

We will look at domestic violence and assess how both customary and statutory laws guiding marriage have fared in preventing the use of brute force in settling domestic or family disputes.

Unwritten Cultural/Religious Laws and Domestic Violence

Culture and religion dictate how families are run in Nigeria. In Northern Nigeria, there is no distinctive line between culture and religion. Due to the fact that the Northerners are predominantly Moslems, their attitude to life and domestic violence is measured by Islamic religious standard. The Islam religion advocates love for one's spouse. However, those that can afford to marry more than one wife are admonished to love them equally and "beat" them mildly. This is anchored on the fact that, in Islam, women and children are considered as persons under the care and protection of the men. They are considered to be under men's care in the sense that they should be molded and disciplined when and how it is necessary. This, though, does not amount to license for abuse and infliction of grievous bodily harm. The implication, however, is that what may be considered as domestic violence in parts of Southern Nigeria may not be accepted as such in the North. In the North, the entire practice of matrimonial causes is hinged in tenets of Islamic religion, which is an important part of their culture and tradition. These practices transcend the whole North from Kogi to Borno and from Northern Kwara to Soko-to/ Kebbi states.

In the South, the Igbo, the Yoruba, the Bini, Itsekiri, Ibibio, Ijaw, Isoko, etc, have their cultures completely different from religion. Though religion keeps influencing the ways of life of these ethnic groups but, unlike in the North, one can still see the difference. The culture of these people does not, in any way, encourage domestic violence as much as is the case in the North. But a certain level of physical abuse of a spouse is often justified by the community/society if the person is seen to deserve what he/she got. There are certain forms of domestic violence that are acceptable, depending on the circumstance. Self defense, defense of persons under one's care, as well as the protection of property are examples of acceptable reasons to justify domestic violence, from a cultural perspective.

In Igbo culture for instance, the people have devised means of tackling do-mestic violence without following the legal process or involving law enforcement agents. I will cite two incidents that I am very conversant with. The first was when I was a teenager in my village. A man, let's call him Mr. "A," was fond of beating his wife as a matter of daily habit. No week passed without incident of serious case of wife battering. The priest, village heads and a few others counseled the man, to no avail. And that was a man who could not face any of his mates in a common wrestling bout but who specialized in beating his wife over frivolous issues. On one occasion, he gave the wife a cut in the face, slightly above her eyebrows, thereby causing blood to flow freely. The next morning, the women in the neighborhood (inyom di) assembled in the man's house and beat the man to stupor. They did not stop despite the wailing and cry of his wife that they could make her a widow. The man was hospitalized for two days after the general beating, the type of beat-ing our law classified as mob attack. But the result was amazing, the couple lived, peacefully, ever after. Till the man's death a few years back, he was nicknamed "Joseph" because he was quoted as saying that the lesson taught him by the "mob" action reformed his life such that he and his wife lived like "Mary and Joseph," in reference to the marital bliss of that holy family of Nazareth.

The second was an event that happened, also, in my home town in March, 2010. The man involved, let me call him Chief "B," holds an *ozo* title from my home town of Ozubulu, Ekwusigo Local Government Area of Anambra State. One night, he left his base in Onitsha with a woman (another man's wife) to his house in the village. Although he has his own house that was securely fenced, some women in the big family saw them and promptly made a call to his wife that night and the next morning, by 6 a.m., his wife was at their gate in the village knocking and demanding that her husband should open the gate. Sensing trouble, the husband arranged for the woman to escape through the back fence where he had lowered a ladder for her. Unfortunately, for the woman who was on flight, she was pursued by other women in the extended family. The man opened the gate and demanded that his wife should explain why she left their Onitsha home. Claiming that the wife was falsely accusing him of infidelity, he descended heavily on his wife, beating the confused wife who at that point could not substantiate her claim to pulp, to the extent that she could not stand on her feet. Unfortunately for him, the women that pursued the fleeing lady came back with the promiscuous woman. The man got deflated and sensing that he is in trouble tried all he could to appease everyone at the scene but the incident was more than he could cover. First, the community took over and after stripping him of his *ozo* title, he was given 14 days within which to appease the wife and come back for other rituals to appease the land and possibly restore his title. He did as demanded by the customs and today peace reigns in the man's house. His wife has since taken advantage of the incident to be in total control.

The two cases cited above are not hypothetical cases. They were real and they were treated in accordance with the unwritten traditional laws. One thing about the traditional ways of handling domestic violence is that it is dynamic. Although precedence is followed, it comes with modification in its application, depending on the circumstance and persons involved. The second case cited involved a Chief, an enlightened big man from the city. If the community had supported the women to use the same method used in case number one to deal with case number two, it might not succeed because the man is strong enough to defend himself from the physical attack of women. The man is enlightened enough to call police to arrest his attackers. So the beauty of traditional laws is its dynamism; it continues to change as society evolves.

In some customs, especially in western and northern Nigeria, the society will frown on a woman who dare challenge her husband over issues like the one cited above. In the early twentieth century, I doubt whether it was possible for a woman in Igbo land to have the audacity to challenge the sexual escapades of her husband. But things are changing; the influence of Christian religion that proposes one man one wife and the sanctity of marriage, which has found its way into Nigeria's legal system is, in large measure, responsible for this change. We will look at the received English law, the Marital Causes Act, and see how it seeks to prevent domestic violence.

Domestic Violence and the Marriage Act

Nigeria, on gaining independence from Britain in 1960, adopted the English Legal System in all its ramifications. The received English Law then came up for ratification before the various Regional Parliaments and thereby became enforceable in those regions where it has been so ratified. However, this was enforceable only to those that freely opted for it. It made the administration of the laws guiding marriage difficult. However, where the provisions of the Marriage Act were not clear on a matter under litigation, recourse is usually made to common law for a way out.

The Matrimonial Causes Decree of 31st day of January, 1990, the Laws of the Federation of Nigeria, Volume 12 was promulgated after the Law Revision Committee, under the chairmanship of Honorable Mr. Justice G.B.A Coker (retired Justice of the Supreme Court of Nigeria) came up with final document. This was the effect of reviewing and harmonizing several enactments and subsidiary legislation of Matrimonial Causes in Nigeria by the Committee.

When the military came into power in Nigeria, they tried to unify the entire marital laws by promulgating the Marital Causes Decree which seeks to centralize the laws guiding marriage in Nigeria. This was the harmonization of the various marital laws in the region with the proviso that it applies only to those that opted for it. Under the Regional Marital laws, as well as Marital Causes Decree marriages conducted in churches and in accordance with Christian religion is regarded as one conducted under the Act. Much later, legislation was enacted making it compulsory that, for a person to be said to be married under the Act, the person must undergo the process in the Marriage Registry in the Local Council Area.

It was not until the Fourth Republic, under former President Olusegun Obasanjo, that the Matrimonial Causes Act Cap M7 and Marriage Act Cap M6, Laws of the Federation 2004 came into effect. This harmonized version has, Marriage Act of 31st December, 1914, Matrimonial Causes of 17th March, 1970 as well as other enactments and legislation incorporated in the 2004 Act.

The question is: What is the provision of Marriage Act, as it concerns domestic violence. Since the amalgamation of the southern and northern Nigeria in 1914, there has been law in place guiding the marriage institution. Provisions which are still enforceable today outlined Offences and Penalties under the Marriage Act. Offences like false pretense, marriage to one who is already married, fictitious marriage, impersonation, marrying minor or under aged persons, etc, were all punishable under the Act. But conspicuously absent are the provisions and penalties for domestic violence.

One, naturally, would think that domestic violence should form the basis for dissolution of marriage but that, again, is absent. Section 15 of the Marriage Act, Laws of the Federation of Nigeria 2004 stated eight provisions each of which is enough ground for a decree of dissolution of marriage. This is contained in section 15 (2) (a-h) of the Act. None of the provisions expressly recommend domestic violence as a reasonable ground for dissolution of marriage.

However, section 15 (2) (c) states: "The court hearing a petition for a decree of dissolution of marriage shall hold that the marriage has broken down irretrievably if, but only if, the petitioner satisfies the Court of one or more of the following facts: (c) that since the marriage the respondent has behaved in such a way that the petitioner cannot reasonably be expected to live with the respondent;"

No doubt, domestic violence, by virtue of the above provision, is enough grounds for dissolution of marriage because anyone visited with violence or threats of violence repeatedly is not reasonably expected to continue living with the other party.

Apart from the above, offenses against human persons, such as the infliction of grievous bodily harm and its related offence, have been taken care of in our laws in both criminal and civil enactments. In the circumstances, as it relates to husband and wife in civil and to some extent criminal procedure, it becomes complicated because the law, all over the world, treats husband and wife as one. This principle, otherwise known as human unity, has absolved spouses from liabilities in matters that the opposite would have been the case if the principle of human unity was not applied.

One example is that a man cannot be charged for raping his wife because the conjugal right is deemed to be expressed when it comes to a man and his lawfully married wife. The man, though, may be charged for indecent assault but not rape. A wife cannot be liable for an offence she committed in the presence of her husband, except when it is a case of grievous bodily harm and murder. A wife is though a competent witness but not a compellable witness against her husband in a law Court.

From the foregoing, there is overriding need to effect some changes in our laws to tackle the challenges emanating from modern family set up. Express and deliberate legislation on areas of domestic violence is very important. In most countries, jurisdiction of the Court to handle issues concerning marriage celebrated under the Act is vested in the High Court. This is good but attention should be paid to those who cannot afford the services of an attorney. The way the churches and the society see divorce needs to change because there is no sense in being in a marriage where domestic violence, unhappiness, and the possibility of a tragic end is imminent.

On Why Nigerians kill their wives

The issue of femicide, as it concerns Nigerians in the US, has become very worrisome. Honestly, this matter should be thoroughly dealt with, for I do not understand why killing one's spouse or oneself should be considered a solution to marital problem for those involved.

Cases of marital problems, such as divorce and domestic violence have been attributed to finance, infidelity, insubordination, etc. In America, a woman is given rights, protection and privileges that she can enjoy and possibly exploit to achieve a selfish end. The statistics suggest that 97% of divorces in the US are initiated by women. The law favors women and they are willing to use it at the slightest provocation and opportunity, leaving their spouses frustrated. Sometimes the frustrated man goes to the extreme towards solving his problem, hence the incident of femicide as in the case of Iheme, Emeruwa, Akeredolu, Ojukwu, Omorogieva, Okafor and Olufemi. The above are the most recent cases, two of them within a space of two days in August, 2010. It was reported by Lilac Hammer that 500 Nigerians are in prison for mostly femicide. This is the first time I am coming across the word femicide. What we Nigerians are accustomed with is culpable homicide punishable with death, as applicable with Penal Code of Northern Nigeria or murder as in Southern Nigeria Criminal Code. The Americans were able to isolate this to distinct it from other cases of murder.

Honestly, I am not against divorce; because divorce certificate is better than Death certificate. The moment one does not have respect for one's spouse, as to treat him or her with disdain, that marriage is better done away with, otherwise one will be burdening oneself with guilt.

It seems some Nigerians go into marriage in America with Nigerian mentality. In America, marriage is a social contract while in some other places it might be "till death do us part" In America, I learnt that over 40% of marriages ends up in divorce and if that is so, I do not see why any American, whether immigrant or not, will think that his or her marriage is made in heaven, as the Priest erroneously made them believe. Someone asked me, how can divorces in America be avoided? And Ezeani Achusim in one of his pieces answered that, "a lot of the divorces in the US could have been avoided if the two never got married." But what if the couple has children? The question that people easily forget is whether the children are better off in a household where love is absent between the parents, or on their own, with or without either parent? Remember that there are social safety nets available for children, should their parents become incapacitated. I have read a divorce case where a man met a lady at a club and the two decided to go home together. The next day they decided they should get married. Two months later, one of the couple asked the other while sharing drinks and cigarette in an ordinary conversational state, "can you give me a divorce?" the other responded "why not, when do you want it, we can still be friends" the lead speaker retorted "good, talk to your lawyer while I talk to mine" The two have same mentality over marriage.

Was it not Mazi Odera who once wrote that "your life happiness ended the day you took your marriage to a judge or the day you get yourself a divorce lawyer; that was the day you wave bye-bye to your joy and happiness." Any person with the above notion understands marriage in its traditional sense and may not lose sleep over what some will use their guns to settle.

From the forgoing, it is clear that there are two schools of thoughts, the one that prefers divorce certificate to death certificate and the other that believes that with divorce life becomes tasteless and valueless.

Let us face the fact that, with few exceptions, the only woman that truly loves you is your mother. She is the only one that will not deny you under any circumstance. This is a fact that our wives will never admit. I want to "hammer" this into your subconscious so that it becomes a living experience. Any person with this kind of mentality will never resort to violence, in case of the unexpected. If you have this in your mind, you will not be keeping evidence of suspected infidelity against your spouse because, once you start doing so, you will end up using it. When you start counting errors against any person, you start losing your affection.

Dan was right when he argued that femicide is not in our (Nigerian) genes and culture. It is not in our culture because we consider marriage a serious institution, as well as sound spiritual knowledge that guides our everyday life.

The question is: What is the solution to this husband killing wife image that now hangs on the neck of every Nigerian, as if with a thousand fetters? Those that kill their wives did not understand what they did and as such they should be seen with pity. They lack the knowledge which I will disclose.

People have to accept situations they find themselves, particularly if they can't help it. By this I mean accepting the fact of life. Have the courage to accept things that you cannot change. One has to prepare one's mind for any eventuality. That is why you see men in their forties writing their Will and Last testament. These men accept that death can come at any time and have to prepare for it; they are realistic. This means that for two things one will happen; it is a matter of time, either dead or alive. So in marriage, either the marriage succeeds or it fails, and so one has to prepare oneself on this at all times.

To be honest with you, if I have evidence of infidelity against my wife, for example, I am not sure that I will go for divorce and I will not give her a laurel wreath either. If my wife should tell me that these my children that are clearly my photocopies are not mine after all, honestly no one will hear it, I will not fight over it and in the next few months in the same neighborhood a young woman will be carrying my baby. It is as simple as that. I may have sounded very raw and a bit unrealistic but that is the kind of mindset one should have to cope with such challenges.

The X factor that could lead one out of the chaos of the present day confusion that has engulfed many marriages is that admonition: KEEP THE THOUUGHT OF YOUR HEART PURE, once this is done immediately bad thought flashes in your mind it will be met with the pure thoughts that repels violence. In fact, with pure thoughts, darkness must retreat and evil on the flight. So one has to discipline oneself by practicing self control in that once you think of taking any action that will amount to revenge, violence, etc., you should say in your mind: I dissolve this for it is false or God forbid or over my dead body or, as Pentecostal Christians will say, I bind this in Jesus name and so on, that quickly dissolves the thought.

If someone tells you that he saw your spouse with one man/woman and that the way they are sitting was suspicious, ask that person and so what? Be honest with yourself and your friends. A friend of mine told me that his daughter called her and demanded that they should see immediately. It was the time he should be at the clinic attending to patient but because her daughter sounded worried and he asked her to come over. The daughter came complaining of her husband who has suddenly changed; how he stays late night and so on. The man in low voice sympathized with his daughter but trivialized her complaint by telling her that boys must be boys. He surprised her by telling her that those things he is accusing her husband of doing he (her father) did so when he was younger. With opened mouth and shining eyes she cleaned her eyes and went home. She has been the best of wives to her husband despite her husband's weaknesses and her husband reciprocates and I am sure that marriage will never know any pain.

We should be honest with ourselves in that there is no one without fault. One may have a larger sexual appetite than the other; one may be more extravagant than the other, and so on. In such situation, the couple should try to hit the middle point by adjusting. The moment you start counting errors and keeping tabs, you are in for unhappiness. However, when issues became out of hand, heaven and earth will bear you witness that you did your best. For violence of any kind, it has never been fashionable and it will never be.

In an extreme bad case, spiritually speaking, the one murdered is not really put in any disadvantaged position, at all. I will not go into that without digressing. It is hoped that we will all learn from the bad experiences of others.

Chapter 4

Igbo Wife in America - Profile

by: Evelyn Nwigwe

Discussing the daily activities of a typical Igbo wife living in the United States of America will start with discussing her overall interest as a person. Human beings like to accomplish certain things in their lives, such as getting education, housing, vehicles, money, children, love and, above all, good health. A typical Igbo wife living in the United States of America works hard to get education, job, maintain her family and offer financial assistance to people she left back in Nigeria. Achieving these goals is important to make her to feel accomplished, as a wife. The question is, how does a typical Igbo wife in America juggle her daily life in order to accomplish her set goals?

In order to understand the mindset of a typical Igbo wife in the US, in terms of what she intends to accomplish, I asked Favor, a good and close friend of mine, to discuss what she does from when she wakes up to when she goes to sleep. Favor, to me, is a very nice and dedicated young woman. I met her when she first joined her husband a few years ago. We became friends and have been friends since then. Prior to her coming to America, her husband, Etoka who also a friend, traveled to Nigeria, married Favor and brought her to the United States to start a family. Favor respects Igbo culture and believes strongly in Igbo traditions and ethics. She makes sure that she speaks Igbo to her children and that her children know where they come from, by taking them to Nigeria every chance she gets. Favor has stated that she makes sure that her family comes first in everything she does.

This brings me to looking at the "profile of a typical Igbo wife living in the United States of America." It is difficult to discuss the lives of all the Igbo wives in the United States due to the fact that each wife has had different experiences than others. However, because Igbo culture stresses the importance of family and stipulates that married women should take care of their families, there are bound to be experiences that these women would have common, particularly in terms of how they perceive their daily roles, as housewives. For example, most young Igbo women coming to America, either to join their husbands or as single women would aim to work hard, get education, raise family, and save enough money to help the people they left in Nigeria. That's the typical mindset of the typical Igbo wife living in the United States of America. To this extent, my friend, Favor, fits a typical Igbo wife living in the United States of America. Her short narrative of her daily activities appears to mirror what you find with most Igbo wives living in the United States of America.

Speaking with Favor, she stated that when she wakes up in the morning, the first thing she does is to pray with her husband. She is a good Christian. Her children are still too young to join in their morning prayers. She stated that she would start introducing the children to the prayers, as they get older. Favor shared that after morning prayers, she would go straight to the bathroom and take care of her hygiene, before she goes to the kitchen to prepare breakfast for the family. Since the children are still young, she prepares separate meals for them, including a special dish for the baby. Favor and Etoka would have breakfast, separate from the kids. Favor has three children, ranging in age from one to five years. She said that she is lucky to have a husband who is willing to help her with housework. She claimed that while she makes the breakfast, her husband, gets himself ready for work and the children ready for school and daycare.

After breakfast, Etoka takes the children to schools on his way to work while Favor would stay home and clean up. Then, she would go to sleep because, as a registered nurse, she prefers to work nights so that she can be there for her children during the day. When she wakes up from her nap, usually before noon, she would prepare lunch before picking up the children from school. Favor, also, shared that she is studying, online, for Master of Nursing degree. She stated that the degree would help her make more money and work fewer hours than she is currently working. According to Favor, "I am very lucky because my husband helps out." At the back of her mine is the fact that some Igbo men would hold onto their cultural beliefs that women "must do all the house work, including raising the children." This belief is an accepted behavior in Igboland. It will be added here, though, that there are a great number of Igbo men living in the United States with their wives who are also helping out with household chores.

Most Igbo wives in the United States don't have the luxury of having house helpers. One reason for this is that it is hard and expensive to bring a child from Nigeria to join the family here, as a house girl or houseboy. When women engage in "women talks," they often share their experiences among themselves about how their husbands help out or don't help out around the house. Helping out around the house is something a typical Igbo wife living in Nigeria gets, easily, from house girls and houseboys and not from their husbands.

These house helpers, sometimes referred to as house-girls or maids and houseboys, would do almost everything for the new wife, starting from the first time she arrived at her new home, her husband's compound. Initially, she may not have "maids." In that case, she would have to take care of everybody in the compound, including her husband's parents and everyone else in the household. When the new wife wakes up in the morning, she would start with sweeping the compound, cleaning up the kitchen before making breakfast for the family. If there is no water in the house, she has the responsibility to fetch the water before it is time to prepare lunch, again for everyone in the house. This part of her married life gives her new family the opportunity to evaluate the type of wife she would be. At this time, the family is watching to decide whether to like her or to start criticizing her and complain to her husband that she may not be a good wife for him. In many cases, the husband does not pay attention to the family's complaint. Instead, he would continue to enjoy his new wife. As this goes on the new wife's family of origin will watching how things are going and would start thinking about how to make life easier for their daughter.

It is customary for the wife's family of origin to find a house girl for their daughter, to help her in her new home. Also, in order to cater to the needs of her husband, the family or the new in-laws (wife's family) would find a houseboy for the husband, as well. This arrangement is quite different from what a typical Igbo wife living in the United States of America would experience.

In Nigeria, after the new family is established, with the husband, wife, apartment, house girl/boy, etc., the wife would have little or nothing to do in the house, compared with when she first arrived in the family. She would not sweep the compound or clean the kitchen any more. She may not even prepare any meals because she now has a house girl who does the house work for her. The houseboy also has his own duties, catering to the needs of the husband. It is the houseboy's duty to fetch water, fetch firewood, where applicable, and wash the husband's clothes. The difference between the daily activities of a typical Igbo wife living in the United States of America and that of her counterpart living in Nigeria is that the Igbo wife living in Nigeria has a lot of help from the house helpers and, sometimes, neighbors, compared to her counterpart living in the United States of America. In most cases, for the Igbo wife in America, her husband is all the help that she has.

Speaking with Favor and some other Igbo wives, one would conclude that Igbo wives in America have no choice but to find the strength and stamina to carry out their day-to-day activities, which include working different shifts, attending school, taking care of the family and attending the series of weekend functions that Nigerians host on weekends. Her counterparts in Nigeria have no problem attending any function they wish to; after all, they have most of their housework done for them by the house helpers.

Typology of Igbo Wife

Basically, two categories of Igbo wives living in the United States of America. I'll classify them as the dedicated Igbo wives and the self-centered.

The Dedicated Wife

The dedicated wife goes to any length to protect and care for their families. This wife comes across as the manager of her household. The dedicated wife is in charge of the family's finances, education, healthcare, housing and overall well being of the members of the immediate family - her husband and children. The dedicated Igbo wife, from my observation, attends events with their husbands and children well groomed. From my observation, also, some of the dedicated women engage in healthy completion in many things. For example, they compete in who dresses her children better and who has better cars, houses and more education. It appears that this competition drives the women to work extra hard, in order to achieve what they want and meet the goals they set for themselves. It has been observed that some Igbo husbands are also involved in the management of their family affairs, in support of the dedicated wives.

Many of the dedicated Igbo wives were lawyers or teachers in Nigeria who got married and moved to the United States to live with their husbands. These women decided to change their careers to nursing and related health professions, based on the fact that nursing would help with gainful employment. This category of Igbo wives help their husbands take care of their children and other family members.

The Self-Centered

On the other hand, the self-centered Igbo wife exhibits behaviors that raise tension in the home. She is the type of wife that concentrates attention only on herself. She also works hard and makes money. However, she likes to keep the money for herself. She would make her husband provide for the family and would not extend any kind of support to the husband's family. She would secretly send money and other materials to her parents and siblings back home, without the knowledge of her husband. To avoid trouble, her husband may allow her to keep her earnings.

It should be noted that the self-centered wife is not common in the Igbo community in the Diaspora. The average Igbo wife living in the United States is dedicated to the welfare of her immediate family and would go to any length to work and help her husband run their household. She does this by paying their household bills and making plans for the future of their children. In addition, she makes sure that they live in their own home instead of renting. In many cases, the dedicated wife and her husband will even make joint arrangements to build a house for the family at home (Igbo land), if that is needed. They both work and decide on how many children, from the husband's family, they will help through school. With that type of "good wife," the husband is always willing and happy to support his in-laws. The husband will not mind inviting his in-laws to visit them here in the United States because he has a wife who supports him.

Passing the Torch
One good thing is starting to take place with Igbo wives in the United States. There appears to be a socialization process in which some younger Igbo wives have started to learn from older Igbo wives who have set good examples. For example, the older wives who have raised successful children, and who have not instigated any explosive family problems, are informally mentoring these new Igbo wives. The result appears to be that there is less family problems nowadays, following these mentoring programs among Igbo wives in some parts of the United States. The affected Igbo wives appear to be paying more attention to their children. Even when they have to work many hours, they still make time for the children. A friend of mine now works only three days a week, so that she can use the rest of the week to "hang out" with her children. It appears to help the children a lot, particularly where the man of the house is also involved with the children.

When the children know that their parents are there for them, it makes a lot of difference in terms of the children's behaviors. Children like to look up to their parents for good behavior. When the mother is working long hours and the father is also working, leaving the children in the care of babysitters, the children usually develop behavior problems because they know that their parents are too busy to care. In essence, to maintain a good and happy Igbo family in the United States of America, both the wife and husband must be in collaboration in supporting and providing for their family members both here in the United States and in Nigeria.

Cultural Dissonance?
The two categories of Igbo wives living in the United States of America may have different understanding of Igbo culture where married women are regarded

as members of their married families. The dedicated wife understands that and helps to make her marriage work. She brings harmony in the family by being very understanding and helping her married family, financially and otherwise. In most cases, the family with the dedicated wife rarely experiences domestic violence that sometimes leads to divorce. Conversely, the self-centered wife, who concentrates in taking care of herself and her birth family tend to behave in ways to raise tension in her married family. There is evidence that most of the serious marriage problems and divorce within Igbo marriages in the United States are, in part, due to the manner in which the wife conducts herself in the family. Men can also exhibit behavior problems that sometimes lead to serious problems in the marriage. Igbo marriage counselors are now stepping in and helping Igbo marriages in the United States to re-direct the couples to remember where they come from and the cultural norms that should guide conduct in their marriages or families. It is important that Igbo wives create positive environment for the next generation of Igbos living in the United States of America. To attain this goal, it is imperative that Igbo couples always remember to respect their culture and seek ways of maintaining unity and peace in their marriages.

Chapter 5

Taking Responsibility for My Marriage

by: Brown Ogwuma

Every culture has its own fair share of marriage failures and divorces, for one reason or the other. It is possible that problem marriages are more prevalent in certain cultures than in others for particular reasons. I believe that failed marriages and divorces will remain a feature of the institution of marriage. For one, marriage is a union of individuals who bring a mix of good and challenging baggage into it. In other words, people are, generally, unique and different and so are partners in a marriage. It becomes a problem when the rate of divorce or failed marriages go up dramatically or when relationships degenerate to the level in which partners kill one another.

As stated in the title of this piece, parties to a marriage must know their roles and responsibilities in the relationship and make every effort to play those roles effectively. They must also bring goodwill, good faith, and trust to the union. Of course, it is essential that parties to a marriage develop common interests and goals. These interests and goals, for the most part determine the success or failure of the marriage. Frictions and infractions in a marriage imply conflict, which requires a resolution and that the partners are committed to resolving the conflict. Whether marital or otherwise, to be able to resolve a conflict, parties involved need to understand the various sides to the conflict. Ordinarily, it would appear that there are just two sides to a conflict—your side and the opposing party's side. However, there is a third side, which is the correct side of the conflict. It is also known as the middle ground. A willingness to understand and hear these three sides - your side, the opposing side, and the correct side/version is advised. Incidentally, people generally tend to see only their own side of an issue. Introspection, the ability for insight and identifying personal lapse and acknowledging it, is a depth that is not easy for people to attain. Knowing that there's something to change about oneself is a good indication that the person is ready to make necessary change in behavior. For change to occur, it is imperative for someone to be uncomfortable with where things stand at the moment, envisage a desired future, and then proceed with making the necessary change.

Across the cultures of the world and of the Igbo, in this instance, it's taken for granted that people get into and stay in marriage. Often, people go into marriage without knowing that it is something about which they need a vision and an expectation and that it is an institution that the partners need to build and nurture. And like any other structure, there are building blocks for a marriage. It is also important to recognize that people are different and unique which also makes each marriage to be different and special. Every marriage turns out to be a product of what the parties involved put into it. The building blocks implied here are the characteristics of the parties to a marriage. These building blocks include values, knowledge, understanding, vision, judgment, etc. Having a successful marriage requires the parties involved to grow in it by being able and willing to understand, respect, and accommodate each other. Furthermore, it requires adaptation and compromise. To be able to do this requires that the partners share common value and goal about the marriage.

My interest in and commitment to writing this book is better captured in this expression: *"Onye g'igwo aku nmuo ya tifuta mpisi aka ya."* This expression is an Igbo adage in Ngwa dialect. Translated in English, this means that whoever professes to treat whitlow should stretch forth his finger to show that he has suffered one in the past. This is about showing that one has experienced the ailment that one professes the ability to treat. It is about showing proof that one has worn the shoe and know where it pinches. The finger is supposed to show the scar of the healed whitlow, as proof that one is fit to heal others. The aku nmuo (whitlow) here is failed or problem marriage—the subject of this book.

I have personally gone through a marital problem, and then a failed marriage. When the invitation came for me to contribute to the writing of this book, I accepted without hesitation. Headline news in the mass media of Nigerian couples killing each other in effort to resolve marital squabbles inspired this project. My personal experience did not go as far as the murder of a spouse. One reason for this is that the issues in contention were not that egregious. Another possible reason is that the temperament and personalities of both or one of us did not let it go that far. By the way, I narrowed down the issues in that marital conflict to divergent values, personalities, and temperament of my former wife and me. I was the one that took steps to end that marriage. Stemming from that experience and after the dissolution of that marriage, I conceived of and started a survey of African families here in the U. S., with intent to create a supportive, cultural-sensitive program that would benefit people going through marital problems. Moving on with my life following the dissolution of that marriage, I have since remarried and now reside with my current wife who joined me here from Nigeria eleven (11) years ago. I feel good enough to state that both of us live not just amicably but as best friends, also. This has made a world of difference for both of us.

So, as I make my contribution towards writing this book, I stretch forth my finger, as proof that I have been there - where some others are right now in their marital lives. I could empathize with them and, hopefully, through this work, help any or some among them to get a better perspective on marriage and also get a grip on their marital issues.

The Cost of Conflict

As a Clinical Social Worker, just like Mr. Aliche, my co-author, my area of work is the human services. One critical and core focus of this field is human behavior in the social environment. Two terms used to express factors that play into what a person does, how s/he behaves or who that person becomes, behaviorally or otherwise, is "Nature and Nurture." The later, Nurture, is about the environment where the individual is raised, its attributes, and what it has to do with who she/he does become. This includes learned behavior or the influence from others. Conversely, the former, Nature, speaks to innate, genetic, and/or heredity factors that shape the person, influencing what he/she does become. Generally, individuals have little or no control over things in this realm, as they seem to be pre-determined at conception. One way to get some insight and work on this is through education and marriage counseling.

Essentially, at the core of this subject is conflict, albeit marital conflict and how to resolve it. Although the bout of conflicts afflicting Igbo marriages here in the United States, some of which have resulted in husbands murdering their wives, is driving this book project, the problem is not limited to Igbo marriages and couples. To the spouse who murders the other—the husband, in those cases captured in the documented news stories, killing the spouse might seem to serve as a resolution. However, in reality, nothing is resolved. Yes, the murdered spouse may not be around to continue bringing whatever factor s/he was bringing to the conflict-ridden relationship. The surviving spouse, the children from the marriage, and even extended family members on both sides would still be mired in conflict, intra-personal and inter-personal conflicts. That surviving spouse would face legal problems and the stress that go with it, particularly here in the United States, a country of laws. In many, if not most cases, that spouse would be jailed for many years. If this does not constitute a living hell ruining his/her life, I don't know what would. Most likely, the children would have difficulty dealing with the shock, trauma, loss, and grief of this tragic and sudden loss. At some point, it could trigger mental health issues, such as acting out behavior, depression, etc. On the inter-personal and inter-family levels, the two families could be trapped in deep sense of loss and grieving plus, possibly, blaming one another for having something to do with the tragic turn of events.

One thing to point out is that, although more husbands kill their wives here in the United States, wives do kill their husbands too. Aliche did cite some statistics from the United States Department of Justice for the year 1994 showing that about 1,400 wives were killed, while 680 husbands were.

Marriage – Do they know what marriage is?

Consider this entry about marriage in *Wikipedia*, the online dictionary:

"Marriage (or wedlock) is a social union or legal contract between people that creates kinship. It is an institution in which interpersonal relationships, usually intimate and sexual, are acknowledged in a variety of ways, depending on the culture or subculture in which it is found. Such a union, often formalized via a wedding ceremony, may also be called matrimony.

"People marry for many reasons, including one or more of the following: legal, social, libidinal, emotional, economic, spiritual, and religious. These might include arranged marriages, family obligations, the legal establishment of a nuclear family unit, the legal protection of children and public declaration of commitment. The act of marriage usually creates normative or legal obligations between the individuals involved. In some societies, these obligations also extend to certain family members of the married persons. Some cultures allow the dissolution of marriage through divorce or annulment.

"Marriage can be recognized by a state, an organization, a religious authority, a tribal group or local community. It is often viewed as a contract. Civil marriage is the legal concept of marriage as a governmental institution, irrespective of religious affiliation, in accordance with marriage laws of the jurisdiction."

I personally like and chose this definition of marriage because it is broad and nearly all-encompassing, covering aspects of reasons people marry; including culture, value, social, legal, religious, physiological, libidinal/sexual, etc. A close look at the variables here that impact and underlie a marriage, requires that partners/ couples navigate and manage them well in the interest of a successful marriage. Is it any wonder why conflict rears up and derail many marriages? This is more so given that even identical twins are anything but identical, in many instances, especially in personality, character, temperament, and even value.

My sense is that many, or even most, people do not have this much grasp of what marriage entails or the variables to contend with, in their union. One reason is that marriages, especially the first time marriages, are executed at a relatively young age. Personally, I did not know much of these facts; much less understand their implications for a marriage, at the time of my first marriage. And speaking of reasons for marrying, one reason that seems to factor into marriage in Igbo culture, and some other cultures is economic. In our Igbo culture, particularly in earlier times, and in recent times too, men are not only expected to pay bride price on a bride, they are expected to provide for and take good care of their wives. The implication here is that they should elevate the socio-economic status of their wives. And also, they're even expected to elevate that of their spouse's parents and family. With this as the focus, almost other things like peace of mind, happiness, cordial relationship, and mutual respect become secondary. Conversely, some wives, particularly of late, now come to their matrimonial homes with the goal and an objective of propping up their own family of origin, even at the expense of their family of marriage. Such wives act as ambassadors of their family of origin, representing it and serving its interest, while in their marital home.

It is important that spouses create enabling environment in which a couples can grow in their marriages. Growth here is about learning more and becoming wiser with knowledge, over time; understanding marriage better; its place in their lives, and its implication for priority setting. One other way is for yet-to-marry individuals to think ahead on what they want and expect in a marriage—the value they place in a marriage; learn the pitfalls in marriages and the way to navigate them for the benefit of their families and offspring.

Both Nature and Nurture can exert influence on marriage at the same time. Clearly, factors like value, culture, family and social roles, for instance, are environmentally and socially driven. Conversely, where mental health factors, including depressive disorder, mood disorder, and schizophrenia, for instance, combine with situational and environmental factors, things can be complicated. Note that factors of temperament and personality could be attributable to both Nature and Nurture.

Having pinned down the contributory factors to the failing of my first marriage to contrasting values, personalities, and temperament, let me proceed with a focus on the formal definition of these factors.

Value

Value influences the choices people make. They are things that people hold dear. Some values hold steady as others change in consonance with structural shifts in the greater society. In a society where things are better grounded, broad and transparent values permeate the climate, forming the basis for good faith, which is essential for effecting transactions (culled from Root That Binds; Brown Ogwuma, 2005).

In ethics, value is a property of objects, including physical objects as well as abstract objects (e.g. actions), representing their degree of importance. (Wikipedia).

Personality

Personality can be defined as a dynamic and organized set of characteristics possessed by a person that uniquely influences his or her cognitions, motivations, and behaviors in various situations. The word "personality" originates from the Latin persona, which means mask. Significantly, in the theatre of the ancient Latin-speaking world, the mask was not used as a plot device to disguise the identity of a character, but rather was a convention employed to represent or typify that character. (Wikipedia).

Temperament

In psychology, temperament refers to those aspects of an individual's personality, such as introversion or extroversion that are often regarded as innate rather than learned. (Wikipedia).

With the basis and background to this chapter explained thus far, the supportive theories and facts to it are laid it in these categories:

The place and benefit of Courtship before marriage and possible drawback to not courting.

Compatibility of Partners/Spouses

Culture and its influence/place in a marriage

Mutual and Reciprocal Respect

Handling and Managing Money

Sex, It's Satisfaction and Fidelity

Partnership: Working it out and Managing it

Values, personalities, and temperament

Divorce: An option or Not

The place and benefit of courtship before marriage and possible drawback to not courting.

One could question the place of courtship in a marriage's success or failure, considering that in the United States courtship is the norm, yet, marriages fail all the time. This is more so with statistics showing that more and more Americans are divorcing or staying single. This does not warrant dismissing courtship on some level and any positive contribution it may bring to a marriage. Culture could and does make a difference in the health or survivability of marriage among Africans on the one hand and Americans on the other.

From my experience growing up, courtship was not the norm in the Igbo institution of marriage, as it implied friendship and sexual relationship outside of marriage between two young unmarried people. At least, it was not openly encouraged and accepted. While such (sexual intercourse) could be tolerated with single men, it was rather objectionable for single women. Back then, single but old-enough-to-marry women with notoriety for promiscuity had difficulty attracting suitors. Any girl noted for pre-marital sexual activity would have her chances of marriage within her community and its environs severely reduced. While this may not have applied across the subcultures of the Igbo, it did apply in mine. I recall some matured girls in my early elementary school years who would slap boys for hounding or pestering them for friendship. Any such boy who dared to strike them back drew a swift beat-down from a gang of boys.

Further back in time, many marriages were purely arranged. Arranged marriages included those that parents on both sides arranged for their children, even from childhood. The parents, virtually, seal the marriages for their children, and would want a daughter-in-law who is much younger, in the home of the future "husband" who would grow into womanhood in that household. Often, the fathers or even the mothers involved in arranging marriages for their children are friends who want the relationship cemented on a long term basis. Some other marriages are initiated at the recommendation of relatives of the would-be couples. This very much obtains today. Usually, the man initiates the search for a bride and relatives assist by recommending girls who they know to come from reputable families. The primary criterion here is good morals. Other criteria may include self-sufficiency and good behavior. Unlike many of today's marriages, those arranged or recommended marriages endured, apparently because they were anchored in the culture and tradition of the people. As the culture is predominantly paternalistic and male-domineering, the wives mostly played along "knowing and staying in their place." This, I would say, is what held such marriages together. Many marriages that started with recommendations still work out, do well, and endure, partly because those who recommended the marriage often intervene when any form of tension or conflict rears its head.

There have been instances in recent years where the move for recommending potential wives has been questionable. This is often seen in the recommendations made by relatively young relatives of a suitor; where the basis for recommending a spouse-to-be is not quite thought out. Many of these instances of abuse of the recommendation culture have happened where men residing overseas are involved. In one of the case that has come to my knowledge is when a female relative recommended her friend whose character was questionable. The two friends are school mates but know little or nothing about each other's family background, which normally is the main basis for recommending or making those matches. The thing that makes this match making non-traditional or even selfish is that the motive is to link one's friend with a good catch, someone with good economic and in social status. Marriages built upon this kind of origin have a higher chance of failing, compared to ones in which the good character and reputation of the bride to be and that of her family is the basis for recommendation.

Indications are that parents are fast losing their influence when it comes to a decision or the process leading to who their daughters will marry. During a trip to Nigeria in 2008, two young men, single then, had remarked that many young women desperate to marry would readily move in to live with a young man and any young man, as long as the person agrees to let her moving in. The feeling or opinion of the girl's parents or family carries little or no weight in this circumstance. In a culture that requires bride price and other payments by the suitor, some of which are elaborate, girls are said to ignore their parents' demand for huge sums of money and other expensive materials, in an effort to avoid missing an opportunity to marry. So, girls in Nigeria appear to be threading the path of their counterparts in the United States and Europe, who basically follow their hearts when marriage is involved.

In the United States, conversely, a marriage goes ahead whether or not parents have a say in it. In many cases, all that the young couple may do is go before a Judge or the relevant government official to seek and get a marriage that is captured in a signed document, usually a marriage license. The would be couples could court from anywhere from weeks through months to years and may reside together for as long as they pleased. In doing so, the couple may have as many children as they pleased. For some reason, the signed legal document or marriage license carry an overriding weight.

Many marriages, irrespective of how long courtship lasted, fail due to the incompatibility of couples and their expectations from marriage. In the case of the Igbo in America, some fiancés and spouses join their partners just to come to the United States and/or help to prop-up their own families. Such girls come with the expectation that living in America holds the key to getting whatever material things that they want. Some have been known to accept marrying any man who is able to bring them over even when their true intention is to get an opportunity to run to a boyfriend who is already here and who they very much fantasize about. In some cases, they learn the hard way that either the man who brought them over or the boyfriend they planned to meet is married to another woman or is doing very badly, economically. Some even get the rude awakening that their man is living the life of a criminal.

Considering the acute need for couples to understand one another well before committing to a marriage, the place for courtship before leaping into marriage cannot be overemphasized. In this context, courtship serves to not only educate one about the other, it also offers the opportunity to mutually adapt and be accommodative of each other where that is an option for both or either. Where both or either see no room for change or are unable to bridge their differences, it is only reasonable that a decision not to go ahead with a life-long commitment that marriage entails be made. Moving forward with his/her life where this becomes the case, the individuals involved would have no significant regrets, having benefitted from 20/20 foresight that s/he chose, as it were.

Compatibility of Partners/Spouses

That economic considerations drove many Igbo marriages is not in doubt. In that male-dominated, paternalistic society, a women marrying into "wealth" simply had it made. As in many areas of life where things are changing and adapting to the times, people should consider other factors, when thinking about who to share the rest of their lives with. Couples-to-be should seek and strike a chord of compatibility, to give the marriage a good chance of succeeding.

Take age, for instance. To be able to provide well for his wife, economically, the husband has to be working with reasonably steady income. It was a given, therefore, that he was much older than the wife who would be insecure without a husband able to reasonably meet her and her future children's economic needs. The problem with basing a decision to marry mostly or solely on the economic factor is that it makes it difficult to consider compatibility of the parties involved. To break this down, one has to see the fact that partnership of marriage requires sharing life with all its tribulations and challenges. Partners need to ponder this and the way(s) to navigate these challenges. In life also, there are stages of growth and even regression, not just physically but mentally, spiritually, socially, and otherwise. With one spouse in the middle or nearing the end stage of life and the other at the beginning (the Genesis and Exodus, metaphorically borrowing from the Christian Bible), is it inconceivable that the spouses may not satisfy the other's needs, including sexual needs? The point here is about working to strike a balance that has a better chance of producing a happy marriage.

There are cases in which once or twice-divorced older men marry woman as young as their children and brag about it. And this is despite certain red flags, some of them obvious, that such marriage may fail. It turns out in some of the cases that their very young wives have either used them to come to America or that the two do not match in age, knowledge, experience, and interest. Yes, age does play a role in those areas. And when it comes to marriage, youth, beauty, and sexual attraction are good qualities to look for but those should not be at the expense of compatibility. A wide disparity in age can drain and derail a marriage.

Culture and its influence on marriage

The institution of marriage is impacted and shaped by cultures, across the societies of the world. I do believe in culture. One with no cultural identity can be said to be adrift or afloat. That person would not be anchored. The definition below gives credence to the above statement. It's a definition of culture from Wikipedia-on-line: "An integrated pattern of human knowledge, belief, and behavior that depends upon the capacity for symbolic thought and social learning."

It is critical to note the components of culture: integrated part of human knowledge, belief, and behavior ... that depends on the capacity for symbolic thought and social learning (Wikipedia); even at the risk of being repetitive.

As critical as culture may be, people still have the option to make a determination on which aspect of a culture to embrace. One reason is that culture and tradition seem to change constantly. Historically, traditions emanate from practices handed from one generation to another and continued down the generational line with the intent that they survive over time through practice. However, somewhere along the line, however, every generation would have a way to invent new traditions or practices to serve personal or sub-group interest.

To bring this to bear on the subject of marriage, consider the fact that in Igbo culture, across the board, marriage is not just a union of the spouses; it is also a binding of the extended families and communities on both sides. For the most part, this is good. A bad side to this, however, has been that some close members on either side of the families have over-stepped their bounds and roles by dictating to either of the spouses what to do, to the detriment of that marriage. This issue, to my knowledge, seems to have played out in some of the Igbo marriages that have failed here in the U. S. I'm persuaded to say that one solution to this is for the spouses to grow up and step up to take control by keeping an overly intrusive extended family member in control. To be able to do this, one has to have the capacity to dissect and analyze the issues. It is about you, your life, and interest; remember! Of course, that family member may be the father or mother who raised you and has been one great and indispensible ally of yours. But when it's time to take charge of your marriage do it!

On the traditional roles of the husband and wife, it is important to make necessary changes, too. To the husband who would still expect the wife to cook all the meals and do all the cleaning in the house, don't forget that roles have gone through shifts and adjustments in the "modern" homes and families. There are hardly stay-at-home mothers in this shifting and changing environment. Probably, your wife works to enhance the income of the family. This would mean that it does not squarely fall on your shoulders to meet the family needs, even if it had at some point. Actually, there are instances where husbands have become the stay-at-home partner. The point here is simple: husbands, be ready and willing to learn some of those chores and help do your part to get them done, if need be. And wives, that you work and bring either some, most, or all of the income does not necessarily exclude you from also doing your part of the chores.

Mutual and Reciprocal Respect

Mutual and reciprocal respect for one another is the cornerstone of a successful marriage. Respect is critical for one to feel good. As modern marriage is significantly a partnership; only those who lack the insight to notice the changing trend would still carry on with the old school way of marriage, to the detriment of that marriage. Below are some of the things that have changed about the marriage institution:

Polygamy is waning in many cultures, as not many men have the economic power and the influence to hold a large family together in this practice that has little or no consideration for the feeling of every individual wife.

Women are as educated as, sometimes more educated, than men in modern times. For this

reason many wives make as much income, and sometimes more than their husbands.

I see respect as being about each partner valuing the contributions of the other partner to the marriage and of partners validating each other. As one good turn is said to deserve another, validating your partner would very likely lead to that partner doing more to the benefit of the union. Where there are no reciprocal respect among partners, marriages would fail and deservedly so. If the spouse who is on the side of mutual and reciprocal respect is seen as naïve, it's good to remember that this is your marriage and people are different, unique, and distinct in many ways. Another thing to remember is that marriage is a work-in-progress, particularly in the early years. In addition, there are lessons to learn and one should be open to learning in this process. It takes the naïve and well-intended to initiate collaborative and beneficial efforts and, eventually, build trust.

Although it cannot be quantified, respect is one of those invaluable qualities many cultures value and which individuals crave, because it brings out the best in many good-functioning and well-meaning people. Yes, you deserve it and so does your spouse and marital partner. If the excuse for not respecting one's spouse is that the spouse (wife) is much younger, and this is mostly the case in Igbo marriages back in the days, one thing that should be clear is that when a couple, married or not, consummate their relationship/marriage sexually, that age line is very much blurred, almost not existing anymore. For the husband who places too much value on being put on the "worshipped" pedestal by his much younger wife, get a grip and grow up. Your wife should be your friend.

Handling and Managing Money

"Money is important, but it's not everything." This is one of three statements by my current wife in the period that we "courted" that endeared me to her, as I felt that we share three chore values. Among other things, those values—the other two I hope to share later—prompted me to go forward with the marriage. So far, over eleven (11) years later, it has turned out, so far, that I was not wrong with the move.

Money may not be everything for my wife and I but it's a central issue in many broken or failed marriages. Talk of value and the misplacement thereof! There's no question that money is a sensitive issue in marriage. I was having a discussion, about two years ago, with an older man in my community who has been married for decades, with their children all grown up. The discussion topics included how I make decisions to spend money on my wife's side of the extended family and mine. When I told this man that my wife and I discuss and agree on what to spend and how, he seemed astounded. He then asked me: "You mean that you discuss with your wife every expense you would make on your side of the family?" Hearing me respond "Yes," he retorted "Good luck!" Does this not imply that I was headed on the path of a slippery slope?

Pondering over that, later, I wondered who is in a better position to know the potential pitfalls in a marriage than one who has apparently been successful at it for about 40 years. Then I reassured myself that people are unique and different and do not have to adopt the same approach to things to be successful. One thing I have learned and always reminded myself about marriages is that if the way people handle issues in their marriage works for them, whose place is it to question that? They don't have to do it the way my wife and I do it in our marriage. That my wife and I discuss and make those decisions and it has worked for us for a total of 11 years makes me happy, irrespective of what others may think of say.

In the years of my first and failed marriage, another older man in my community who professes that he likes me and my family had a reason to share with me that his wife handles most financial transactions of their family. He said he had to yield that role to her as he has confidence and trust in her money handling ability. Implied in this confidence and trust is that they shared a value of a common marital goal. The point here is that, with shared values and common goals, spouses should be willing and ready to yield roles in the areas they have identified the other to be better. For the success of the marriage and family, couples should learn to enhance and complement one another and grow together. Hopefully, they will pass those values to their children who would learn from them, imbibing and passing same to their own children. A saying in Igbo culture, Ngwa dialect, goes thus: *Nne eghu d'ata, umu ya d'eleya anya l'onu*. In English: While the mother goat chews, the baby goat watches her mouth for what they can learn.

This speaks to modeling a behavior. Although they also learn from listening and hearing, it's been shown that watching and observing what parents do is the more effective way that children of impressionable age learn.

Sex; It's Satisfaction and Fidelity

Sex and sexuality is a sensitive subject matter in Igbo culture, even among married couples. Discussing the subject openly is like a taboo. Anyone who discusses the subject openly is generally castigated for being out of line with the norm. As a result, sexual issues or disputes amongst a couple would simmer and corrode the relationship. I do assert here that the sexuality in humans, like in lower animals, is biologically driven and inseparable in their nature. Yes, it takes a cultural norm to get a handle on sexuality and bring some decency to it. But cushion it all we can, the need and place for sex needs to be validated.

For married couples, recognizing and acknowledging this need and a partner's role in helping the other partner meet the need cannot be wished away. In many cases, there will be differences in attitude to sex and sexual intercourse between the partners. One source of this difference is how a partner dealt with sex from her family of origin growing up—openly or discretely. One may need more of it, while the other needs less. This could be determined by their respective levels of sexual drive and awareness. It would seem that the Igbo culture, with varying sub-cultures thereof, has a position that the woman is subtle and not overt in expressing her sexual interests and desires.

Exacerbating factors to avoiding sex could include exhaustion from work or other energy sapping activities. This becomes an issue when a woman uses these factors as excuse to withhold sex in marriage. There has been cases where a wife would withhold sex, punishing her husband as it were, for not getting her way or things she thinks she should get from him—money, clothes, or otherwise. A related phenomenon is that there are wives whose husbands do not satisfy them, sexually. The reason here may range from waning sexual drive/prowess of the husband due to illness or aging. The factor of aging, particularly where the age disparity between the husband and the wife is wide, with the husband older of course, brings back in focus the compatibility issue

Again, is it inconceivable that a much younger wife would have more sexual drive than her much older husband? On the other hand, it can only be expected that a man headed downhill in his life cycle will, inevitably, do so with his sex drive. Yes, men may reproductively active longer that women, and fathering children much later in their lives, yet when it comes to sexual energy, old age is not favored.

Couples need to know the factors that potentially contribute to decline in sex drive and what they need to do to address their negative impact on their marriage. They should find out if this is what the affected spouse has any control over. What is needed is for the "well" partner/spouse to support and encourage the other to do and follow through with things s/he could do for remedy. In cases where exhaustion is the issue, the sexually-denied partner learns to understand and empathize, while the denying partner learns to accommodate the sexual need of the other, as much as is possible, under the circumstance. With both getting to understand better the place of sexual intercourse in a marriage, and that providing it is a duty the spouses owe each other, they would be able to reach the necessary middle ground.

Failure to do this could and has led to infidelity by one spouse. While the inability of a partner to meet sexual needs may not be the sole reason to cheat, it can be a contributing factor to infidelity and should not be overlooked. There may be people who cheat for a variety of reasons. Removing a potential excuse by taking steps to meet sex needs within the marriage would not hurt. This is about showing your spouse/partner that you understand and care, not just in other areas, but when it comes to sex, too. If all would face it, partners in a marriage need to open up and be genuine about sex. Being real and genuine is not about throwing decency in the wind.

The norm, in any culture, has influence and impact on marriage in different areas, including sex. In the Igbo culture, and in the context of the sub-cultures thereof, it would not be much disputed that women are expected to suppress their sexual feelings, at least in my generation. This being the case, getting a respected woman to be responsive to overtures by men was usually difficult. And, for women to initiate sex, you might as well forget about it. Imagine, then, the culture-shock that some of our young men who came to study in the United States in the 1980s felt with women and sex in the southern parts of the country, as captured in these two brief instances:

One friend told a story of his American girlfriend who, seemingly, could not get enough of sex. She not only wanted to have it at every opportunity, night and day, she would seek him while he's in school, to the extent that he considered leaving the city for her. He told of how the girlfriend would make him withdraw more money at the ATM due to distraction, as she performed one sex act or the other on him, He used to tell us that he was "losing his mind." He said that these were sexual acts that he least expected from a girl.

The second story was from another friend who would most mornings come to my house to stay until the evening, in order to get away from his girl friend, who incessantly wanted to have sex with him. Linda was a student in another college and was also on summer break at the time. One of the comments this friend made at the time was that he never imagined a woman being this open and obsessive with sex. Unlike my peers and friends at the time, I was married to my former wife a few months before I left Nigeria to the United States, and had brought her with me, which was unique at the time.

Partnership: Working it out and managing it.

Impliedly or clearly stated the word partnership reverberates through this chapter and cannot be overemphasized. This is because it is what modern marriage should be about, in order to succeed. The reality underscoring and driving this is the social and economic paradigm shift of the times. Like business partnership, marriage partnership is about growth, strength, and reaping the attendant benefit by pooling resources together. While this benefit may be financial with business, in marriage it's about the enhancement of the couple and the family. It is really personal on a different depth—intrinsically the lives in, and that of the family. As with business partnership, the partnership of marriage should have a vision, mission, and goal, from the on-set. Again, cultivating goodwill and good faith is critical for the success of the marriage. Dealing in goodwill and good faith brings about trust. And transactions between individuals that lack trust would wither and crumble. Playing games with each other for reasons of lack of common interest or incompatibility is one sure way to derail a marriage. Instead of putting up fake fronts, one might as well seek to exit the marriage. Building a trust through goodwill and good faith could start from one spouse. Although the other partner, either by his/her nature or otherwise, may not reciprocate on time or ever, the partner who provides an opportunity for building mutual trust should be proud of themselves. The spouse who takes the lead here needs to have no regrets doing so, whether or not the other spouse reciprocates. Granted that some people will try to convince that partner that he's being taken advantage of, he or she should not give up. Knowing that one knows what one wants in one's marriage and taking necessary steps to achieve it is all that one needs to be concerned about.

Also, as the saying goes, all work and no play makes Jack a dull boy. This is about really making efforts at finding fun time together. It may take being creative with jokes and things that amuse you both. I must say that this is working for my wife and I. We have now created an array of words, slangs, and phrases that we routinely use to infuse some humor into our relationship. We have made it a habit to call one another at work, at least, twice during a work day. This has really become a second nature for both of us such that we feel like something is missing until one calls the other. And we express to each other the desire to get back home from work to be together; meaning we do miss each other when apart for several hours.

Working together supportively and in a mutually-enhancing manner in a marriage brings about synergy. With synergy, people with common interest and goal achieve more than they could individually. One expression used to articulate this succinctly in business education would be two (2) plus (+) two (2) equals (=) five (5). A partner needs to know and do what it takes to enhance the partnership, helping it to survive, thrive, and succeed, all things being equal. As with many things in life, not all partnerships work. If a partner has done what he or she needs to and the partnership must fail, seek to pull out of it the way that makes sense. It's not worth wasting a life.

Values, personalities, and temperament

Having identified that disparity in values, personality, and temperament between my former wife and I ensured the failure of that marriage, I beam a little light here on these factors.

That one spouse highly values certain things and the other does not, whether derived from one's upbringing or some other factors could and does pose a challenge in a marriage. Take money, for instance, as critical as it is to life and living, it's neither a panacea for a successful life nor for marriage. Growing up, I did hear that, in one sub-Igbo culture, they have a saying: From wherever money comes in, let it come in. Stated differently this means that The end justified the means. Contrast this value with the value of my Igbo sub-ethnic group value that emphasizes self sustenance in food—not depending on another for a basic primary need to eat and be fed—and living honorably.

In the above two scenarios in which values are expressed, one would explore and exploit any channel, legal or otherwise to meet that highly valued end. On the other hand, the other would avoid tarnishing the highly valued honor, but focus on first meeting the basic of needs legitimately. Hence, Money is important, but it's not everything.

"Personality can be defined as a dynamic and organized set of characteristics possessed by a person that uniquely influences his or her cognitions, motivations, and behaviors in various situations." Given this definition, personality has a high potential to impact a marriage and other relationships. For marriage, which is about the most personal of all relationships, compatibility of the partners and being able to manage any differences in personality is critical to success. Being a partnership of a very personal nature, again marriage requires a vision, goal, and

61

action plan. Some may not have had these ingredients from the beginning, as many start it at young age, driven mostly by culture and attraction or "love." For it to endure, however, partners have to grow in it or face downward spiral and disintegration.

Temperament, the last of the three, is another innate personal characteristic that very much impacts relationships. Again with marriage, the temperament that partners bring to it can make or break it. The disparity in the partners' temperaments and their ability to understand it and manage it will make a difference between failure and success. Two important things to point out with temperament are introversion and extroversion. With introversion, an introvert tends to be private and think through things before acting on them. Doing so, he/she avoids impulsive mistakes and pitfalls. Conversely, an extrovert likes to be noticed, sometimes wanting attention to the point of desiring center stage of attention obsessively. Also, seeking and "hugging" center stage do come with unwarranted competition. Extroverts tend to show off and prove to others that they are doing better. Even with things as simple as clothing, the extrovert wants to wear the most recent in the community. When he/she feels or thinks he/she's unable to so prove, he/she would blame their spouse, the husband here, mostly. As husbands, traditionally, are expected to be the family providers, she would see him as a failure and blame him. The thought and relevance of how much income is earned and the opportunity and the circumstances that spouses have had in this American society—education and otherwise—matter not. Another thing she might do is spend her portion of the family income trying to meet and satisfy this need, drastically raising the heat of disagreement in the marriage, as they do so. The husband could in turn blame her for squandering the household income on things she does not need.

When I decided to re-marry with a goal of finding a woman potentially of identical values with me, one thing that I set out to do was find one from my sub-Igbo ethnic group. Doing so, I knew that this criterion alone was not enough for a marriage to succeed. After all, I knew of marriages that failed, even though the spouses came from the same sub-ethnic Igbo group. My first wife, though an Igbo, was of a different sub group. I reasoned that one good way to narrow down possible incompatibility with a future wife could be to look internally in my own sub-ethnic group. This is because sub-ethnic groups share identical values across the board. This being so, chances are that a wife within the group would have a good chance of imbibing many of those common attributes and values. And after 11 years of this marriage, I believe I made the right decision.

Divorce: An Option or Not

If every marriage works out well or be salvaged and saved, divorce then becomes irrelevant. Ideally, every marriage should be successful. The reality is that marriages do fail. In fact some marriages have failed so badly that some Igbo husbands in the United States have had to kill their wives, one of the reasons that prompted work on this book. Didn't we advertize long ago that this book project is about saving Igbo marriages?

Although divorce has been a feature of the marriage institution in cultures across the world, it is a feature and fact that the Igbo wish will go away, putting it mildly. The degree to which sub-Igbo groups detest divorce varies. It depends on the values within a sub-culture. Here is an instance where one would consider divorce:

A woman, of my sub-Igbo group, who has been married for several years and has always resided in Nigeria with her husband and adult children, has issues in her marriage over the years. A critical examination of some of the issues shows that the underlying issues are value based. She saw her husband as one prone to criminal lifestyle for monetary gain. Also, her husband has unfaithful; cheating, going out with women to the knowledge of his wife, etc, instead of diligently and intelligently doing what needs to be done, to achieve material success. On her part, the wife decries and discourages those. The husband then moved in with a woman with many children who is a diviner/seer in his new-found church, leaving his home, wife, and grown children. A friend of the woman suggested that she divorces this husband for bringing disgrace to her. The woman rejected it, adding that she would even fight it if her husband initiated it. Her reason was that this would entail that she returns to bearing her maiden name; which would imply that she's unmarried or really divorced. This underscores that she values being married and staying married, almost at all costs!

Mending the Roles that Came with Man In the State of Nature

No matter how many times it is repeated, the need for knowledge, insight, making changes and being adaptable in roles and other areas in a marriage for it to succeed cannot be over emphasized. In Igbo and some other cultures, men are seen to be dominant and subjecting women to the background in marriages. This is the basis for many to conclude, without looking into and analyzing the facts, that problems in Igbo marriages here in the United States come about because women/wives have chosen emancipation over subjugation while men/husband still stand to stifle and repress them.

With the case for couples to make the necessary changes made, throwing light on the origin of the "male domination" would not hurt. In fact, it could help. The term "Life in the state of nature" is not unfamiliar. Typically, it refers to and describes conditions of humans and their lifestyles, dating way back eons ago, and before advances in knowledge that have brought about the changes and advances of today. In that state, the male by nature generally is physically bigger and stronger and the female more supple, being effeminate by her nature also. As if this fact needs proving here, my wife and I were, recently, watching a TV program featuring a wildlife expert who was studying the life and socialization of a particular specie of a large animal in the forest. As a pack, apparently a family of that animal, approached a road intersection and paused, a minute or less, one of them, in front of the pack, jumped across to the other side and turned, facing the rest of the pack still on the other side. Immediately after what seemed like a gesture from one animal, the rest, including the young ones, followed suit and jumped. Narrating what had just transpired, the expert explained that the male had taken the leadership to venture over the other side of the terrain, and signaled the rest of the family to join him because it was safe to do so. To this, my wife stated: the male is the head of the household everywhere, even in the animal world.

And so, with humans dating back to those earlier times for survival, the male went out and about hunting, killing, and gathering food and provided security and safety for the family that included the female and her off-spring. The man also, in a society of humans that progressively became organized over time, was in charge and in control. The woman, of course, is naturally endowed with nurturing instinct and ability to nurture; hence she stayed home taking care of the family and the off-spring.

If not for anything else, understanding, empathy, and partnering in a marital relationship demands that necessary changes are made in the modern human society of today's world. Those having difficulty with this reality and in adjusting, accordingly, still live in the world of the past or in the state of nature. If they could, they're better off growing. Doing things suggested in this chapter may not be enough to salvage your marriage but it should help, significantly.

Chapter 6

The Trouble with Igbo Marriage (1)

by: Stella Nwokeji

All names used in the vignettes are fictional. However, the stories are from real life situations. Identifying information has been removed to protect the confidentiality of the individuals involved.

Marriage in Igboland is a covenant of mutual respect between two individuals, a husband and a wife. It is a complex process that involves both families and sometimes, the community. In Igboland, marriage is a step by step process which is not only ceremonious but lengthy. For some, it may take weeks, months, or even years. However, the majority of the ceremonies can be accomplished in a few weeks. Marriage is an expected union that binds the couple with both families of the couples. This is why an Igbo girl leaves her family and is regarded as her husband's asset. Traditionally, the girl should be welcomed into her matrimonial home with open hands. However, this may not be the case and the results of the deviation from the norm have been linked to marriage problems.

MY IN-LAWS ARE RUINING MY MARRIAGE

Njideka is a forty-six-year old lady who lives in the United States of America. This is her twenty-first year in the country. She is married to Dan who is sixty-years old. The two met twenty-three years ago when Dan was on Christmas vacation in Nigeria. They were introduced by a mutual friend. Interestingly, it was love at first sight for the two. Dan left Nigeria for the United States after his secondary education. His parents sent him overseas to further his education. On arriving in the United States, he did some odd jobs before he got admission into a university. Dan studied banking and, immediately after his graduation, was retained by one of the banks where he did his internship. He worked for the bank for a year and enjoyed his life as a single man. Shortly after, his parents started calling for him to return home and get married. Despite the fact that he had stressed to his family that he needed to work a little more to save money and build a home in the village before marriage, they did not listen. They continued to pressure him until he decided to visit home to consider their demand.

A week after his arrival in Nigeria, he was introduced to his future wife. Njideka, is a pretty lady from a middle class family. She is the third of six children of a teacher (father) and a housewife (mother). Njideka finished nursing school two years prior to meeting Dan and had worked at a local hospital in the city. Although she thought about marrying someone from overseas, it was not her main concern. However, upon seeing Dan, she fell in love with him. After a few trips and disappointments at the U.S Embassy, Njideka received a visa to come to the U.S to unite with her husband. A year later, they were blessed with a baby girl and, subsequently, two other children will follow.

Dan and Njideka enjoyed their married life together. Njideka would get her nursing license after her third child. The couple was comfortable and able to take care of their children and extended family. Dan and Njideka's problems started when Dan's mother got a visa to come to the United States. Dan had filed for his mother to visit after Njideka's mother came to visit three times during the birth of their three children. Dan's mother in-law's three visits have created a problem between Dan, his mother, and his family. Dan's family believed that his mother should come for one of the "omunkwo" (a period when a mother visits her daughter immediately after child birth in order to help her recuperate). Njideka was not happy about it. However, in an effort to please her husband, she accepted her mother in-law's visit. This was the beginning of marital problems between Dan and Njideka. Dan's mother seized the opportunity of her visit to Dan's house to renew her controlling tendencies towards Dan and eventually his wife.

IMPLICATIONS

Most marriages, including Igbo marriages, are bound to disintegrate if a third party gets involved in a divisive manner. Here, Dan's mother is the third party and her controlling action is detrimental to the marriage. Some mothers-in-law are nice and treat their daughters-in-law as their own biological daughters. A majority of them tend to transfer the love they have for their sons to their daughters-in-law. However, there are mother-in-laws that are known for their callous and wicked ways. These women are not only jealous of their daughters-in-law who they perceive as a threat for taking over their sons, but are determined to see the marriage suffer. This type of attitude is seen in mothers-in-law who are married into a polygamous relationship. Assuming the mother-in-law is not the first wife of her husband, she is forever not given an opportunity to be the controller of her home. When this woman has an opportunity to visit her son, she tends to take control of the whole environment, not realizing that she has had her own opportunity to play the "madam." In other words, she wants to live her own "missed" opportunity through her son and his wife.

The following suggestion should help you deal with problems associated with mothers-in-law.

Men

A man is the head of the family and should act firmly and gently when it comes to a mother- in-law/daughter-in-law issue. It is a very sensitive and sometimes emotional issue

If you have a mother that is very fond of you and loves you, it is time to let her know that she must transfer the same love to your wife.

When your wife has a child, Igbo culture bestows the honor on your wife's mother to come over, if she is alive. It is not your mother's time to visit and take care of your wife and the baby. Most women are comfortable with their mothers taking care of them during the postpartum period. It is not the time for your mother to learn how to give your wife a bath or massage. You wife may not be comfortable with this idea.

It is okay to look at your mother in the face and tell her that it is not in her place to come this time around.

If your mother has to come to visit you for some reasons, medical or otherwise, firmly let her know your expectations. Your wife deserves happiness in her own home. Your mother's presence should not deprive her of that.

It is okay for your mother to help out in the house if she is capable of doing so.

Gone are the days when women were full time housewives and were expected to have the house and food ready before everyone gets home. If your mother is around and is capable of helping, please encourage her. Your wife's mother will do the same chores for her daughter without her daughter telling her to do so. Helping out with cooking and looking after the kids does not make your mother any less of a woman. It does not translate to your wife taking her as a maid. However, it will foster a mutual and symbiotic relationship between your wife and mother.

If you know that your mother is the provoking or jealous type, you can fly her in and allow her to stay with you for a few weeks. Then pay for her to spend some time with your siblings, if you have any living overseas. Your siblings know her better and can tolerate her more than your wife.

If your reason for bringing your mother to your home is because she cannot be alone in the village, this can be remedied. First, find your mother a maid, provide a cell phone to the maid, and make provision for the maid to live with your mother. Send your mother money periodically for her upkeep.

Remember that your mother has had her own opportunity. This time is for you and your wife. You grew up seeing your father and mother happily married. Why not give your children this opportunity? Why compromise their lives and future because you want to please your mother?

Let your mother understand your wife's role in your household. Your wife should be given the opportunity to manage her family affairs without the interference from your mother.

It is understood that mothers and their sons, share a special relationship. A special bond that your wife may not understand. Subjecting yourself to a situation you want to please both your mother and wife at the same time will be counterproductive. This is because one will always feel neglected by you.

If it is inevitable that your mother will have to live with you and your wife, create a balance between the two women in your life. Carve out time to spend with your wife, have a family time for the entire household, and time for your mother. Some of your time with your wife should not be disrupted because you want to spend time with your mother. It is okay to take your mother out once in a while to make her feel special as well. Trust me, most women will not mind, as long as they are made to feel special as the "madam" of their house. Every woman appreciates the respect accorded to her in any circumstance.

Finally, our mothers suffered and toiled for us to be who we are today. Sometimes, this sentiment overshadows any known faults we know in our mothers. Most times, we deliberately choose not to recognize or acknowledge these faults. In doing so, we follow every advice or suggestions given by them about our wives, even when we know that it may destroy the relationship. Definitely, mothers are precious, but their unconditional love should not be at the expense of your marriage. You must strike a balance between the love you have for your wife and that for your mother. A "familial equilibrium" is needed to ensure normalcy in any household.

Women

It is a known fact that no individual can replace your biological mother. However, when you took the marriage vow, for better or for worse till death do us part, you agreed to love and accept your husband's family.

Yes, some mothers-in-law are provoking but nobody is perfect. You can change her attitude with your unconditional love.

Your mother-in-law is your mother as well. Treat her as you would your mother. Show her love when she shows you hatred. You will be surprised by the impact you will make on her.

Your priority in your marriage is to make your spouse happy. If having his mother in the house is what makes him happy, for the love you have for him, embrace his mother. He will have a different level of love and respect for you.

Even when you find fault in your mother-in-law or she upsets you, ignore the faults and blame it on old age. When she offers you wickedness, ignore it and respond with care.

Ask God to give you the power to overcome the temptation that you are getting through your mother-in-law. Make prayer your priority and hand over all your problems and concerns to God.

Be submissive to both your husband and his mother. Remember that his mother is as old as or even older than your mother. Show her the respect that you will equally give to your mother. Sometimes, your attitude towards a person can change that person for good.

Never lash out on your mother-in-law, no matter how angry you are. Put her in your mothers' situation. Will you disrespect or insult your mother, no matter how angry you are with her?

What if your husband disrespects or insults your mother; how would you feel?

Find out what makes your mother-in-law happy and stick with it. Avoid those things that make her unhappy. Most grandmothers love to spend quality time with their grandchildren. Make that provision for your mother in-law.

Shower her with gifts, if you can afford them. It is fine to get the money from your husband and buy things for her.

If she has other children or daughters/sons-in-law, convince her to go visit them. Ensure her that you will provide the ticket for those trips. Make her see the need to see her other children or grandchildren too.

When she travels, take control of your household. Have a dinner date with your husband and rekindle your love again.

Call your mother-in-law "mother," as you will with your mother. Even if there is nothing to talk about, spend as little as five minutes and ask her how she is doing. Try to keep the conservation going about things she is fond of. Let her know how much you, your husband, and the kids love her.

You gain a lot by loving your mother-in-law and lose everything, including your husband's love, by not loving or respecting her.

Remember, your mother in-law brought your husband into this world, cared and loved him before he met you. There is a special bond between them. Please love her, unconditionally.

You will be a mother- in-law one day, Try and put yourself in her shoes. Perhaps you will understand her better. Think of your mother being treated unfairly in your brother's house by your sister-in-law and feel the pain.

Your husband and children are always in the midst of daughter/mother-in-law issues.

When you have engaged in a confrontational situation, apologize to your mother-in-law when you are wrong. If possible, do so without letting your husband know. Let his mother or others inform him. He will love and respect you more for making peace with his mother.

Finally, no matter how much you feel that your mother-in-law is intruding in your marriage, it is your marriage and you will regain control sooner or later if you handle the situation with care and sensitivity.

WHAT HAS SEX GOT TO DO WITH IT?

In this chapter, the intimacy relationship of marriages will be explored. The graphic description of adults' sexual activities will not be discussed. As private as sex is in our culture, it is an "inevitable relationship." I never expected that I would today be discussing intimacy. This is because of the emphasis that our culture lays on human sexuality. As an Igbo lady growing up in a small city, fairly conservative, sex education was treated as a taboo. Children were not allowed to utter the word sex and even married people kept that part of their relationship sacred and private. Then, adults found it difficult and uncomfortable to discuss sex among themselves. The trend is changing with the emerging civilization. Igbos, especially those in Diaspora, are following this trend. The recent cases and rates of failed marriages and domestic violence among the Igbos in Diaspora have led to questions on what aspects of our sexual and romantic lives are impacting these issues.

Oluchi never expected she would have marital problems because of her sexual life. She has been married to Oko, a taxi driver for twenty-five years. Oluchi and Oko got married in Nigeria, after the two met at a wedding. Oko has lived in the United States for most of his adult life. He visited Nigeria for his cousin's wedding and was introduced to Oluchi by his cousin's wife. Oluchi just graduated from the University of Port-Harcourt and was looking forward to working in Lagos for a few months. Her meeting Oko was welcomed. Both started off to a nice romance for the two weeks that Oko was in Nigeria. Oko left travelled back to the United States two weeks later. Six months after his return back to the U.S, Oluchi joined Oko in Houston, TX with a fiancée visa. The couple married four months later. They were blessed with five children. As the kids grew, more responsibility came up. Oko had to get a second job to supplement his cab driving. Similarly, Oluchi having finished her nursing education in the U.S started work at a local hospital. Oluchi worked the grave yard shift while Oko leaves home about 8.00 a.m. and gets home by 8.00 p.m. He is always at home just on time to stay with the kids while Oluchi leaves around 10:15 p.m. for work.

Ultimately, this couple have wrapped themselves with work and does not have the time for each other. Interestingly, many Igbo marriages have experience of this situation in the Diaspora. What happens to the romance in the life of this couple? People are, naturally, curious about this part of this couple's life. This curiosity is a natural feeling.

Like many women, discussing sex is a taboo and a word not to be uttered outside the bed room. Today, some Igbo women are probably dealing with difficulty discussing sex openly. In fact, many are uncomfortable when it comes to taking the initiative to ask for sexual pleasures from their spouses. This is understandable because of the limited sex education in Igbo culture. Living in the Diaspora, Igbo women might as well get used to sex and its place in their marriages. In western culture today, women are the pillars of the sexual wellbeing of their marriages. Therefore, Igbo women in Diaspora should assimilate and adapt to such responsibilities in other to nurture their own marriages.

According to Durex, sexual wellbeing is "a balance of physical, emotional and sociological factors. It's about protecting and nurturing the sexual health of both you and your partner, getting the most from your sex life, feeling confident and happy about yourself." It is a "fundamental part of human wellbeing and health." In their 2007 Sexual Wellbeing Global Survey, sixty-seven per cent of Nigerians through face-to-face/self completion approach survey said they were fully happy with their sex lives. The same percentage admitted that they engage in sexual intercourse, including foreplay as long as twenty-four minutes. Unfortunately, a year later in 2008, the same survey found that Nigerians are not having enough sex. The study did not attribute the economic situation as the cause, although most people are working long hours and therefore away from their homes due to that. The survey found out that the respondents were just simply tired after return from their jobs to engage any sexual activity. For Igbo couples in the Diaspora, sex, as a "fundamental part of human wellbeing and health," should be taken seriously.

Therefore, the vignette below outlines the strain in marriage when a couple's sexual upbringing and their adopted western sexual ways clash. All names are fictional.

Eke and Oby have been married for three years. Eke is a taxi driver and Oby is currently a stay at home mother. Sometimes, she spends two hours a day at her sister's day care business. Eke and Oby are blessed with beautiful twin two-year-old boys who attend the day care center where Oby works. The couple graduated from reputable institutions in the United States. Eke holds an MBA while Oby has bachelor degree in special education. They reside in Baltimore. Eke has been in Baltimore for more than twenty years and Oby joined him four years ago. They enjoy each other and the support of families, friends, and the Nigerian community in Baltimore. Eke belongs to several Nigerian organizations and is active in almost all of them.

Before Eke succumbed to the pressure from his parents to come home and marry, he was married to Ashley Jones for ten years. Unfortunately, they did not have children. Ashley is a native New Yorker who was attracted to Eke because of his accent. They were course mates at the university and enjoyed each other's company as well. Like many western ladies, Ashley was on top of her game when it comes to satisfying Eke sexually. Eke could sometimes be heard bragging to his mates how blessed he was to have a "sex machine" in Ashley. According to him, "there are never dull moments at home. I get it at the clock and when I want it. Ninety-nine percent of the time, Ashley initiates the moves. It could be in the car, kitchen, bathroom, bedroom, living room, just name it. She is well versed and knowledgeable when it comes to the pleasures of life." Ashley, on the other hand, enjoys Eke's sexual treats to her. Eke's years of living and studying in America has exposed him to what women actually need sexually and he is able to provide those to Ashley, among other things. Eke has revealed to his best friend, Akin, that Ashley always gets emotional when he is tired and not able to make love to her. He explains that "sometimes she goes out of her way to buy new lingerie, believing that I am no more attracted to her. She feels I am bored and she has set several date nights with hotel reservations to rekindle what she feels is low sexual desire in our marriage. She has even gone on her knees begging me to forgive her, if she has done anything wrong to warrant my boredom with sex. On the days I am ready for her; she thanks and appreciates me for satisfying her sexually."

By the accounts above, the description of Eke and Ashley sex life is far from what is obtainable today with Eke and Oby. Eke complains that Oby always uses sex as revenge strategy when she gets angry with him. Unlike Ashley, Oby never initiates any sexual move. Eke claims that he literally had to force himself on his wife in other to have sexual intercourse with her. He claims he is perplexed how sexually deprived Oby could be but yet she will never willingly ask for it. Eke refuses to believe that his wife pretends not to like sex but is convinced that the lack of sex education in their Igbo culture plays a part in her behavior. As a Christian, he is not in any way thinking of divorcing his wife but has had several thoughts of reuniting with his ex-wife, Ashley, even for a one night stand. While waiting for this wife to catch up with his western sexual life standard, the frustration is putting a serious strain on their relationship.

IMPLICATIONS

Even with their busy schedules, Igbo couples can still make out time to enjoy each other and keep the romance going while balancing family and work. Sparks are rekindled when two consensual adults are willing to give it a trial. The suggestions below will help couples in this kind of situation enjoy their sex life while reducing the conflict that arises from a discontented sex life. The key, here, is openness and willingness of the couple to share negative and positive sexual experiences with each other. In addition, expressions of love and care for each other help. Couples should be honest and genuine with what they feel or want in their sexual relationship. It is imperative that such be communicated to each other. As you read the suggestions below, feel comfortable to act upon them or customized them as deemed necessary to fit your lifestyle or improve sexual relationship.

Both Partners

First, start by studying each other's fantasies. Know what is pleasurable for your spouse. Most importantly, elevate each other's ego. A man needs to know that he is your rock, the head of the household, and your love. Similarly, the woman needs to know that she is the weaker sex in the relationship and deserve to be pampered and appreciated.

There is a huge difference between intercourse and sexual relationship. Intercourse is the sexual act while sexual relationship is the intimacy. The later grows marriage and cements the relationship.

To embark on an intimate sexual relationship, bear in mind that reproduction is the product of such act, as well as sexual satisfaction. Sex is meant to be enjoyed. It is an essential part of life, just like the air you breathe or the water you drink. Deprivation from sex can have negative health consequences.

For couples to put spark back into their bedroom, find out from each other your "pressure points". In other words, which parts of your body, when touched, gets you aroused. For women, it could be their breasts or nipples and men their penis or scrotum. It is important you know this for pleasurable sexual experience.

Invest in R rated movies and watch them alone with your spouse while in bed or cuddled on the couch. You can practice what you have watched or try any of the new positions learned.

Sex can start in the kitchen. As gross as this may sound, this is a reality. Your action can set forth the expected sexual activity. While your spouse is preparing a meal or getting something from the pantry, hug, embrace, tickle, or touch him or her sexually to arouse him or her. Naturally, women's brains are wired to build up their sexual urge before the actual act. While your wife is preparing meals, touch or caress her. Show her affection which will build up and prepare the ground for sex. The act may come natural to men without any preamble. However, it is different for women.

You can also start as soon your spouse comes back from work. Simple gestures, such as "welcome back," or "how was your day today? I know you must be tired; can I get you cold water? I took care of the plates, I changed our bed linens today, I took Obi to his piano lesson, today; I put the kids to bed, do not worry; I will take off this and that, to mention but a few, can set the tone for sexual activity later that day or night.

In this age of technology, text each other, affectionately. Although "sexting" is not encouraged, it can also set the ground work for what is expected sexually later in the day.

Engage in foreplay to get the action going and to keep her as active and interested in the act.

Be creative with your sexual activities. Change positions, change rooms occasionally, decorate room with candles and music. Also, when there is help with the kids, check into a hotel and spend a day or weekend, alone.

Find out if your spouse likes light or music during sex. Accommodate his or her fantasy, sometimes, even if you are not comfortable with them.

Know when both of you have reached organism by reading each other's body language. Your main goal is to satisfy each other. Have you done that or did one person feel used or he or she just went through the emotion of having sex?

Read and explore different safe sexual practices and try them on each other.

Attend couples' night out, comedy shows or seminar geared towards relationship.

Once a month, make it a routine to have alone time with each other. Even if it means going to the movies without the kids or having a dinner date.

When you are opportune to attend a conference, seminar or convention, make reservation for a separate room for you and your spouse from the kids. They can have adjacent room to yours. Have a cut off time for most meetings and retire to the room to have precious time with your wife or husband. Order or bring with you a bottle of wine. Drink and relax with your spouse. The next day, you will feel refreshed and have renewed love for each other.

If possible, associate or hang out with much younger couples as a way to keep your marital and sexual life going. Humans learn by emulating others. Hanging around these young ones will remind you of those days when you saw each other as inseparable.

As short as these phrases are, they are powerful. Use them and mean them when the need arises. They can work miracle in any relationship. They are, I LOVE YOU! I AM SORRY!

As a last resort to remedy any situation, consult a marriage counselor or sex therapist. Though it may not be in our culture but it can save your marriage, if the two of you are willing to fight to save it. Remember that, in any marital problem, the children suffer. Your future, your children should not be subjected to emotional pains that result from divorce because of the lack of sparks in your sexual lives.

Men

Women need to be appreciated! Compliment them at all times. Call your wife on the phone at odd times and tell her you love her. Send her flowers or cards at work or school if she likes such gifts.

If you are fortunate to work close to your wife's work location, make out time to go to lunch together at least every other month.

Take her out on the weekends. You can go to the movies or dinner. Build up her sexual drive by touching, hugging, and kissing her. She will come back ready to satisfy you.

Never force your wife into sexual activity with you. Naturally, Igbo women are naïve when it comes to sex, compared to their American counterparts. Your wife can say no to you initially. However, ascertain from her if the no is because of fear of pregnancy, sickness or menstrual flow. If none of these exists, romance her, you will be surprised at her later response.

Never compare your wife with an ex-girlfriend or ex-wife. If you want her to perform to the levels of these women, take your time and teach her.

Find out what she likes and with the kids surprise her with those things.

Every woman wants affection and wants her husband to make her feel like his queen. Take time to acknowledge your wife's positive traits and appreciate them at all times.

Women are like jewel that needs polishing. Your wife needs polishing. Therefore, give your wife money for her upkeep. Do not admire others' wives when yours is at home tarnishing. Make sure your wife dresses up the way you want her to and compliment her when she does.

Take time to let you wife know that she is the most important person in your life. As the mother of your children, she should be made to understand that she is the best thing to have ever happened to you.

All women love a man who is their rock and who will be there for them and the children.

Bear in mind that what works for another couple may not work for you. Therefore, do not discuss your wife's sexual inabilities with your friend. Most times, they are experiencing similar issues.

Women

Most importantly, think back the first time you met your husband, what is it that he admired most about you? Could it be your way of dressing, your hair, your weight, your cooking skills, to mention but a few. Fall in love again by bringing back those things when possible.

Forget all that you know about the only way to a man's heart (his stomach). Yes, this is correct; however, sexual satisfaction tops the charts for all men.

Spice up your sex life. Some of our Igbo men once married or dated American girls before contracting his marriage with you. The competition is on! It is possible that you may or may not measure up but you are intelligent enough to learn. Give it a shot and give your spouse a "sex" of his life, anytime he wants it. Make it con-

75

sistent and you have your man to yourself.

Yes, you have a full time job, you are a full time student, you cook, clean, take care of the kids, attend this meeting or that meeting, scheduled to speak at this women events or the other; it is understood. Granted that these activities are important, satisfying your husband, sexually, supersedes all these activities. Unless you are willing to risk him exploring his desire outside your matrimonial home.

God created men to admire things, especially women. Give your husband sometime to look at. Make your sexual relationship sparkle. No man likes redundancy. Most men want sparks; they want to see you in that "hot wear" looking like a celebrity. Try it for him. It is worth it.

Sex comes with children. Interestingly, that is not the only reason for sexual activity. It can be enjoyable as a pleasurable moment.

Never deny your husband sex because you are angry or he did something wrong. THIS IS NOT ACCEPTABLE. If both of you are angry, try make up sex and two of you will resolve the issue with spending time on it.

Make your home peaceful and clean for intimate relationship with your spouse. All men want a clean environment that they can come home to. If you cannot clean all the time, call the cleaning services and pay for their services. You have little ones or teenagers are not good excuses to let your home go. Cleaning your home and putting everything in order call for a happy man who is willing to satisfy you sexually too.

Make out time to relax with your husband at home even when sex is not involved. Emotional bond is hard to break by any distractor in your marriage if you keep your husband relaxed at home.

Explore his sexual fantasies with him as long as it is safe and endorsed by both of you. Caress your husband, rob his hair, kiss him, and touch him intimately where necessary to get him going.

Men, especially Igbo men, are responsible and as such bear the burden of their extended family. Do not let this discourage him. When he gets those calls, tell him to sleep over them. By sleeping over them, you satisfy him sexually. This will calm his nerve to face any challenge.

Some men use sex as a way to relax themselves. If you have such a husband, count yourself lucky that he is not out there drinking. Why not give him sexual pleasure while you enjoy it too.

As difficult as it may sound, some Igbo men are not experienced sexually. Unfortunately, our culture is to be blamed in part for this. They are not used to foreplay or the affection that comes with sex. In addition, some men due to medical reasons cannot perform, sexually to the optimum. You know your spouse very well and know his shortcoming. Try to encourage him and the two of you can learn together. Teach him, if you have more knowledge than he does when it comes to good sexual practices or techniques. Make him feel that he is the best at it and keep it at that. This is not the time to show your women empowerment degree. He is human and deserves some respect. You may not know this, not satisfying you sexually, hurts him more than it hurts you.

Finally, never discuss your husband's inadequate sexual ability with any man or woman. Nobody has a perfect sexual partner, as nothing in life is perfect. Discussing his shortcoming outside your matrimonial home not only sets you up for gossips, it degrades your once "rock" to a level he may never recover. Like the proverbial parcel, marriage is like a parcel. Whatever you get when you open the parcel, is all you have. Few make good out of their unfortunate parcel while majority are drowned by it.

IS THERE ANY PERFECT IGBO MARRIAGE?

Marriage is a daily obligation by two willing adults whose goals are but not limited to: uniting, enriching, and proliferating the union. Marriage is definitely a complex institution. Igbo marriages in Diaspora are no different and can never claim perfection. Every marriage is unique in its success or problems; the couple involved plays a major role in sustaining the union. As easy as it may sound, each couple's ability to understand and accommodate each other's shortcomings can sustain a marriage. Working through their individual differences and acknowledging their weaknesses are the starting point in a healthy relationship. According to Frank Pittman, "Marriage is like a submarine which is only safe if you get all the way inside." Igbo marriage is no different. The notion that some marriages are perfect or made in heaven is deceptive. Granted, any marriage not built on solid rock of God's grace and divine interventions is headed for disaster. Just as families pray together to ask God for health, long life, and prosperity, a genuine prayer to God to help sustain marriage by families is essential. Igbo marriage in Diaspora is faced with the challenges of families not putting God first or not asking God to intercede in their marriages. A successful marriage is possible, but a stress-free marriage is a myth.

One could ask the question, "Why do other nationalities in Diaspora do better in their marriages than the Igbos in Diaspora, if at all they do better?" Their successes could stem from their ability to hold on to what marriage means to their cultures while incorporating or assimilating the American culture.

To fully understand the outside influence of Igbo marriage in the Diaspora, the following questions and vignettes will be used.

ARE MANY ORGANIZATIONS AND EXCESSIVE MEETINGS RUINING OUR MARRIAGE?

Monica is a thirty-nine year old mother of four who lives in the suburban area of Louisville, Kentucky. She has been married to Diala for more than ten years. Monica is a teacher while Diala is a banker. On a good day, Diala is home by 6.00 p.m. but most days, he is usually home by 8.00 p.m. On the other hand,

Monica teaches at the same school that her four children attend. After her usual classroom duties, she picks up her kids from their school's after-school program. By the time Diala gets home, Monica has helped the kids with their homework, served dinner, and retired to watch the evening news. This has become her routine for almost ten years now. Tonight is different because Monica is tired and she is yelling at Diala when he returns at 10:30 p.m.

What made this good teacher and mother break down in the presence of her children? Monica's story is one that is constantly experienced by most Igbo women in their homes. Apart from his career, Diala is very involved in his Nigerian community, especially in his Igbo Diaspora community. Diala is the President of two different Igbo associations. He also serves as board director of four organizations, and is in many committees for these organizations. Above all, he was recently elected as the chairman of the convention committee of one of the organizations that he serves as a board member. Diala is very busy and Monica understands this. She enjoys the accolades associated with being the "First Lady" of these organizations and the perks that go with it. However, her husband's involvement in all these organizations is ruining their marriage. Today, Kelechi, the couple's first child, had a recital at 6.00 p.m. which Diala had promised to attend. Unfortunately, Diala cancelled at the last minute with what Monica considered a flimsy excuse. However, he had the time to attend a three-hour Igbo meeting that started at 7.00 p.m. The meeting was a planning meeting for their upcoming summer convention. Monica was devastated when she learned that Diala had cancelled on his son just to attend this meeting.

Today, in some Igbo families, men are spending less time with their families and clinging to their social friends in these organizations. Consequently, quality family time is spent away from the family in favor of endless meetings. The purpose of these meetings is no doubt advantageous to our community. However, when it interferes with one's responsibilities to his family, the commitment to the meeting should be reassessed. The worst case scenario is when, at these endless meetings, men discuss their wives and their weaknesses. Advice is exchanged which can be detrimental to one's family. Every family is different and comparing one's family with another can lead to serious marital problems.

Just as endless meetings by men can put a strain on a marriage, endless meetings by women can also affect a marriage, negatively. During the days of our grandparents, women were only allowed to attend kindred meetings and the reason for such meetings was to foster unity among women. Today, an average Igbo woman belongs to three or more organizations; thereby, warranting multiple meetings. Some of these meetings are uncalled for and can easily put a happy family in turmoil. Gossip, unhealthy competition, and infidelity have been known to result from these associations. Also, at risk is the wellbeing of the offsprings of these couples. They are left to fend for themselves. Many are left at the mercy of babysitters. In Igbo land, it is the responsibility of a woman to take care of the family, as well as train the children. When the man and the woman are at two different meetings, who will take care of the children? Who monitors what they are eating or what they are watching on the TV, even how many hours that they have they been on the computer, social network sites or music sites? A fifteen-year-old left to supervise his or her younger ones can easily ignore them while talking to his or her friends on the phone. While mom and dad are at their respective meetings, having fun with friends, cracking jokes, and laughing, they sometimes forget to call home to check on the kids. The irony of the whole situation is the feeling that comes when both husband and wife are home. The former socialites cracking jokes a few hours ago turn into an angry couple immediately they are in their abode. The couple hardly regards each other as partners and forgets that their responsibility includes making each other happy. They frown and condemn each other at the slightest chance.

On the other hand, many may argue that some of these meetings are done by teleconference while the party involved is at home. However, a teleconference that goes on for more than two hours encroaches on quality family time. During the week, families are faced with work, school, and sports to mention but a few. A weekend that is meant for bonding with family is now reserved for meetings and teleconferences. A spouse that follows the trend is definitely risking losing his marriage or even his or her husband/wife or children.

Another problem that plays a central role in an Igbo marriage is the presence of a workaholic spouse. Granted, you need to work in this country to be able to take care of your family. When the number of hours spent at work does not equate to the expenditure at home, there is a problem. Some couples spend the precious hours they need to invest in their family at work. They work their assigned schedules as well as overtime just to make a lot of money to spend on things that may not necessary. Sometimes, our men send money home to invest in business that will never yield dividends, instead of spending the money on their wives and children. They are very sentimental to their families at home instead of making their families in the Diaspora happy and comfortable. Sometimes, some of these investments at home are hidden from the wives who may be contributing fifty percent to the investment, unknowingly. The unfortunate disclosure of any of these investments to the wives by an outsider leads to serious marriage concerns, sometimes conflict.

Chapter 7

The Trouble with Igbo Marriage (2)

by: Stella Nwokeji

SO ADANMA IS NOW IN AMERICA?

Twenty years ago, the numbers of Igbo families with members in the USA were not many compared to today. In almost every single family in Igbo land to-day, there is a family member living in the United States. The pressure to have a family member in the U.S. or to have a financial breakthrough for a family has led to many families giving their daughters away to suitors in the U.S. If the bride is unlucky, coming to America can take two years or more. It can also take less for the lucky ones. If the lucky bride's family is blessed to have their daughter in the U.S, their plans to achieve economic breakthrough starts as soon their daughter is granted a visa. Their prayers are answered immediately they receive a phone call relaying that their daughter has arrived safely to the United States. ****

Ada is a twenty-three year old who hails from one of the well known commu-nities in Imo-State. She graduated two years ago from Imo State University with a degree in quantity surveying. She had worked at a local computer center. Her parents are worried that Ada will not get married because most of her mates are married with at least a child or two. Stanley, a local business man, came to marry Ada, but her family objected. According to them, Stanley is not financially stable. Ada's father is a driver to a politician while her mother is a petty trader. Both have struggled to raise Ada and her six siblings. Ada is the first in her family to attend college. Her younger sister is a second year student at the same university that Ada graduated from. When Ada's best friend told her about a cousin, Chuks, who was visiting home to look for a wife, Ada was excited. Chucks and Ada's brief meeting was love at first sight and they even professed their love for each other. Chucks returned to Nigeria two more times before Ada joined him in the U.S.

Three weeks after arriving in the U.S, Ada received a phone call from her dad who enquired if she had started working. All efforts by Ada to explain her situa-tion and how the U.S system works went to a deaf ear. Soon, Ada's father started calling Chucks asking for money to pay for his other kids' school fees. This was followed by incessant demands for money. In an attempt to please her family, Ada took a job as a baby sitter and hair braider so that she could send money home. Before long, Ada's parents decided it would be fit them to take a chieftaincy title to reflect their new status, now that their daughter lives in America. It was no surprise that they called Chucks and Ada, demanding the sum of two thousand dollars. This was the beginning of marital problems for the new couple.

In this situation, one could think there is a best way to handle this. Unfortu-nately, there is no definite way of dealing with this situation. Love may overpower a man when he is in love and make him to do the unthinkable. However, bear in mind that when a man or woman marries, he or she marries the family as well. The notion of "I will change the family's attitude when we get married," may not be right. A man should make sure he is marrying a wife who is really in love with him. He should be careful of a family is happy to have him as a son in law because of his social economic status or his place of residence. If a man pays attention, he can get important hints about his would be in-laws and their reasons behind their blessings of his union with his potential wife. If, in the process of your investigation or soul searching, you determine that the lady is your wife to be, take every effort to make the marriage work. Never allow your friends, your family, or your wife's family into your personal disagreements with your wife. A third party is not required. A friend who may pretend to be listening and giving your advice may have a worse marriage in his own home. Your family members that you are giving this information about your wife will have a negative attitude towards her. These negative, biased notations may not change even when you come back to tell them about how wonderful your wife is. In involving your family you may have sown a seed of discord which may linger even after you and your wife have reconciled. Men can condescend so low as asking their sisters to speak negatively to their wives or ask them to warn or threaten her after an argument. My advice to a man of this caliber is to grow up, be a man, and handle your own household problems. Your sisters have their husbands' homes to manage and will never see anything good in a wife that has presumably stolen the heart of their brother or in some cases affected their means of getting money from him. Unfortunately, they do not realize that their own sisters-in-law in their husband's homes feel exactly the same way about them. It is a vicious cycle that only prayers, love, determination, and courage can curtail.

SHE MAKES MORE MONEY THAN I DO?
DID I MARRY A WIFE, A NURSE OR AN ATM?

The incidences of domestic violence against some Igbo wives who are nurses has drastically increased in this twenty-first century. Many years ago, Nigeria men could go home, marry a wife they are in love with, and live happily ever after. Not anymore, with the greedy, insatiable desire to make money quick, belong to a particular socio-economic class, and to boost their egos. Today, there has been dramatic rise in the number of Nigerian men who marry nurses. There's also an increase in the number of Nigerian men who want their wives to be nurses. Granted, a career in health care is one of the most lucrative jobs in the United States of America, many Igbo men see it as a gateway to financial breakthrough. Today, the desire to marry someone in a health-related career with the purpose of making money is ruining many Nigerian marriages. Money now plays the critical roles that love plays in marriage. A marriage that places money before love risks a dramatic decline in happiness in that household. The vignette below illustrates a money cautious marriage.

Nkeiru is a twenty-nine-year old nursing graduate of a school of nursing in Nigeria. Nkeiru came to the U.S. six months ago to join her husband. Before joining Vincent, she worked in various hospitals in Nigeria. Vincent, on the other hand, has not held a steady job since his arrival in the U.S. almost ten years ago. It is fair to say that Vincent does not have any formal education that guarantees him a steady job. Sometimes, he is seen hanging around various Nigerian restaurants in the state of Oklahoma where he resides. Nkeiru met Vincent one December when he came home for Christmas vacation. The future of the union started in the presence of Vincent's mother, Ego, who was admitted in a hospital where

Nkeiru works. Nkeiru took care of her. Her tender and loving care towards Ego earned her a recommendation by Ego as a wife for her first son, Vincent. In less than a year later, Vincent and Nkeiru became husband and wife and moved together to the U.S.

Within two weeks of their arrival, Vincent made sure that Nkeiru was up to date with all her immigration requirements. Shortly, Nkeiru received her temporary Green Card to reside and work in the U.S. Vincent stressed to Nkeiru, immediately, that he was not ready to become a dad and was willing to wait until she took her nursing exams, so that she could practice. Nkeiru thought this was unusual, but she was too naïve to understand her husband's true motive. What made it even more difficult to understand, for Nkeiru, is that Vincent is the first and only son among six sisters. Ordinarily you would expect urgency for Vincent to produce offspring immediately to add more males to the family. However, Vincent's sentiment was echoed by all in his family, especially his mother. Nkeiru was lectured seriously by Vincent's mother on the need to make starting a career a priority. In her desire to respect her mother-in-law's wishes and eager to enter the U.S workforce, Nkeiru prepared for her first of two examinations to become a registered nurse. Six months passed and Nkeiru still has not passed any of the exams. Vincent borrowed money and paid for Nkeiru to attend preparatory classes for the examinations. A year later, Nkeiru passed the two exams. Less than a month after passing the examinations, she got her first job as a U.S registered nurse (RN) in a nursing home. Since she was seen as a new graduate who did not have much experience and her starting salary was not much. Vincent did not expect this. Vincent urged Nkeiru to get a second job. She resisted, claiming she was ready to start a family.

In less than three months, Vincent convinced Nkeiru to take a permanent twelve-hour day, five times a week shift. Vincent had made mental division of Nkeiru's first paycheck. It was to be divided into five equal parts, with one-fifth given to Nkeiru. Then, the rest were to go to Vincent for what he referred to as a payment account for bills. Within this period, Nkeiru became pregnant. When Nkeiru received her first paycheck from her twelve-hour shift, Vincent took the money and gave Nkeiru only $100 for her "upkeep". This was the beginning of their marital problems. For years, Nkeiru never got anything more than $120 per her pay period. Sometimes, Vincent went to her workplace and picked up her paycheck. She struggled to deal with the situation while making her marriage work. To make matters worse, Vincent started physically and emotionally abusing her when she asked for more money for her and her baby. He called her offensive names and made statements such as, "I brought you to America and now you are making noise because you are the one making the money," to mention but a few. All these Nkeiru endured because she wanted her marriage to work. She handled her situation within her family. Her Igbo community did not know what was going on. On the other hand, Vincent was seen by the community as the big wig. He made donations at different events, attended various occasions without his wife, bought a luxury car, and took a chieftaincy title from his village. As Nkeiu dies in anguish, Vincent boasts to his friends about how he started building a mansion in his village. While all of these were happening, Nkeiru barely had decent dresses to wear to any Igbo events or enough money to cook food in the house. The compact car that Vincent claimed he bought for her lived in the repair shop most of the time. Nkeiru was forbidden from riding the luxury car or even the SUV parked in the garage. When Nkeiru got a ride from co-worker, Vincent's low self esteem pushed him to accuse Nkeiru of infidelity. The situation that broke the camel's back was when Nkeiru explained to Vincent that she needed to go back to school to get her bachelor's degree in nursing. It was then that Vincent realized that he did not even have a high school diploma. Nkeiru's going back to school was a threat to his ego. To justify his inferiority complex, he told Nkeiru that he knows she will leave him after she gets her degree. The issue of going back to school caused so much emotional pain and physical abuse to Nkeiru that she abandoned the idea.

IMPLICATIONS

The above scenario is happening in some Igbo homes, today. The bible states that a man will leave his family and become one with his wife. Some Igbo men are rewriting this biblical injunction to say and to include the money aspect of their desire; hence, a man will leave his family and become one with his wife if she is a nurse or has money. What happened to our culture when our fathers and grandfathers took care of our mothers, financially, irrespective of how much our mothers made or contributed to the family? What happened to our belief that a man should make the money and take care of his family while the wife stays at home to take care of the children and the home? Women in any society including Igbo society is seen as nurturing in nature irrespective of their financial status. With the advancement today, women are picking up more roles than known traditionally. In addition, education is playing a role on how women perceive their roles as women. It is definitely changing their attitudes, behaviors, and roles in what is considered a traditional Igbo culture. Similarly, the same holds for our Igbo men in our tradition Igbo culture content. Clearly, every Igbo individual or family is definitely unique, however, the suggestions given below may help couples facing the above or related situations.

Men

No doubt, you are the head of the family and deserve respect. However, respect is earned. Before, you travel home to get married, ask yourself this question: do I love her or do I want her because she is a nurse or capable of becoming one?

Just like a man, a woman desires a man who genuinely loves her for who she is. Show your wife love; give her all the pleasurable things of life. If you do this, her pay check will not be an issue.

Get a job and be useful to yourself, your family, and your children.

Be a role model for your children. Show them that you can hold a job. If it is education that is drawing you back, go back to school. There are many options today. You can even work and go to school. You can also complete your degree or certificate program from the comfort of your home, as long as you have access to computer with Internet access. A traditional title is great, but an educated man with a title is even greater.

Do not expect your wife to work twelve hours a day and still run the home, cook, clean, and sexually satisfy you, while you have been on the phone all day or watching TV.

Deal with your complexes or find a way to handle them. No one is cheating with your wife and she is not leaving you by advancing herself through education.

If you treat your wife right, you will be her world and no other man will stand between the two of you, as far as she is concerned.

When you allow her to spend all these hours at work, the little strength she has goes into taking care of the children. Unfortunately, any outside efforts in terms of admiration or financial support can take her away from you in a heartbeat and you are left to wonder why.

You admire Mr. Okoro's family. Yes, he works on his marriage. It has not been easy for him, but he has one trait that you lack—being a real man.

Mr. Okere's wife is classy, beautiful, and educated. Your wife is just like her, if only you look deep down and do your own part to give her those qualities.

Stay away from a lady's purse and/or paycheck. Her paycheck should be a secondary income to your family income while yours is primary. You are the bread winner. Sit up and take care of your wife and children.

If a situation arises and you are not fortunate enough to take care of your family and your wife becomes the provider, appreciate her, and understand her feelings because she is supposed to be taken care of by her husband, not the other way round.

When at home, help clean and cook. It will not make you any less of a man. You are less of a man if your friends know what is happening within your marriage (that's your wife is now the husband of the house financially).

Take care of the children. Drop them off at school and bring them back when necessary. Bond with your children. It is the greatest gift you can give to them and yourself.

Treat your wife to the finest things in life that you can afford. Be spontaneous in your marriage. Spice things up, eating out once in a while and exploring different sexual fantasies. Not only will she melt in your hands but she will take your breath away.

Many men believe that women are incontrollable. Take a moment each day to understand your wife. You have the key to control her.

Some women are hard to please. If you have done all you can that is desired and expected of you to your wife and she is still not happy, you have unfortunately married the wrong woman.

Women

Our Igbo adage states that the pride of a woman is her husband. No matter how economically unstable or even disabled you husband is, if you love him, stand by him. No condition is permanent.

Show understanding for your husband's situation and help him deal with it.

Nagging and telling him how you regretted the marriage will not help the situation. He is a human being with feelings.

If you are the bread winner in the family, count your blessings. You have a job. It could have been worse. Sit down with your husband and discuss what will work for the family.

Yes, it is your paycheck and you worked for it. However, if you entered into the relationship with the hope of living together "till death do us apart," sit down with your husband and map out plans on how to get the family going with one income.

He stays at home on the phone or watching T.V. Help him with his resume. Send in job applications for him, start a business for him, let him go back to school, get people you know to get him a job, and know that you have done your best and given all to the relationship.

Men hate women when they talk down on them. They are groomed, per our Igbo culture, to feel superior to women. Give him that respect. Do not disrespect him. The two of you may be very angry at the same time. Just walk away or stop talking. One has to act as the mature one. Even if you are the younger one, it is okay. STOP TALKING AND WALK AWAY!

Never allow your kids to see you talk to their father in an imposing manner. It is a cycle that will come back to haunt you when they are of age.

See your husband as another baby. You will need to take care of him in addition to your children. Redirect him where possible. Teach him when necessary. Play with him when he demands, and train him everyday. You will be surprised to find out who your favorite baby boy is.

You are a lady; you want the finest things in life, such as laces and shoes, to mention but a few go ahead. However, ask yourself if you can afford them as a family. If you can, go for them. Enjoy life as it does not come with second chances. However, if you cannot, ignore them and wait for your time. It will definitely come if you believe. Everyone experiences the finest things in life, some receive their early while others late.

Keep your work schedule to a minimum. Spend quality time with your children and look into their academics. You admire Carol's children because Carol puts in the time for her children.

Buying laces, driving an SUV, belonging to a particular social club or working twelve, sixteen hours a day, seven days a week is a temporary gratification. Your children are your permanent investment. When the sixteen-hour shift or overtime payment is no longer available or no inflated income is coming in, guess who will be there to console you? Definitely, your children and your husband of course. The social club elites will be the first to disregard you because you are no longer in their "class".

While I encourage staying in marriage to work things through, a union engulfed by domestic violence is not safe for you or your family.

Life has no duplicate. Make the right decision that suits you and your children. Nobody can make these decisions for you. Whatever decision you make, ensure that it is the best decision and that you will be happy with it. Avoid irrational and sentimental decisions, or decisions coerced by friends or family members.

What has age got to do with it?
And, what about Arranged Marriage?

Age difference in marriage dates back years ago when our forefathers married wives that were twice or even three times their ages. Some of these marriages were solely approved and blessed by both families. There are also cases with arranged marriages when the bride sees her husband for just a few days or less before marriage. Today, marital age differences still exist within an arranged marriage. However, marital age differences are declining and arranged marriages are no longer the norm. For many, one or more of these combinations is ruining their marriages, if not their lives.

Ozioma is a twenty-five-year-old. When she was seven, her family presented her with the idea that she will be married to Ibe, a son of their family friend who is studying overseas. Ozioma and Ibe have never met each other. At age twenty-two, after finishing her college degree, Ozioma was told by her parents that she should start preparing for Ibe's final ceremony that cements the two families' long staying relationship. Long before the marriage, Ozioma's mother was teaching her how to cook and clean, thus preparing her for Ibe. After three years, Ibe arrived from the United States. He visited and met with Ozioma and her family twice before he traveled back. Ibe is a soft- spoken fifty year old man who interacted very well with Ozioma's parents during his visits. During those visits, Ibe would boast about his lavish life style in the U.S. Despite the fact that there was no chemistry between the two, Ibe and Ozioma married. Six months later, Ozioma joined Ibe in the U.S.

Reality hit Ozioma when she arrived in the U.S to find out that Ibe has a grocery business that is not doing well. Ozioma questioned Ibe because her parents had told her Ibe traveled to the U.S to study law. Ibe explained to Ozioma his circumstance and how he ended up getting a masters degree in business administration, but never got a good paying job. He elaborated on the fact that it took him years to get his legal residency status in the Unites States. It did not take long for Ozioma to notice that the age difference between her and Ibe was affecting their marriage. It was then that she realized that she did not marry a modern man but a man almost as same age as her father in the village. Most of Ibe's times were spent at Igbo meetings and on his cell phone. The little times he was at home were spent sleeping or watching basketball. He is a very predictable man and eats nothing but his native fufu and soup every day. To Ozioma, she has become like her own mother in the village instead of a wife in the U.S. She got to know the man she married but did not like what she saw. Their sexual relationship was nothing to write home about. Unfortunately, Ibe suffers from erectile dysfunction, which Ozioma was not aware of until a week of non performance that Ibe attributed to tiredness. In the two years that the couple was married, none of them felt emotionally connected or sexually satisfied. With no children and less than three years in her marriage, Ozioma left her matrimonial home to begin life in the U.S. A. as a single woman.

IMPLICATIONS

In a traditional Igbo marriage, a wife is expected to be younger than her husband. However, in Diaspora, the age gap in Igbo marriages is increasing drastically. Some Igbo men wait until they are in their mid or late forties before start making arrangements for their marital future. Others, due to foreseeable and unforeseeable circumstances, fall under this category. Many Nigerian men, after studying in overseas, especially those who embark on prolonged advanced or specialized degrees are usually in their forties before they are married. Although age does not matter, it can play a pivotal role in any marriage. Some Igbo women prefer an older, mature, and responsible Igbo man because of what they stand for. A forty-year- old Igbo man is responsible and ready to settle down and start a family. However, not all men function on this level. Many are still stuck with their cultural identity and lifestyle which can be overwhelming for their new spouses. Below are suggestions that can help both men and women enjoy their marriages, irrespective of their age differences.

Men

Get to know your wife.

You married a young lady. Take time to allow her enjoy her youth; take her on a romantic date.

Eat out when you two can. Fufu is not the only stable food in this world, try other food.

Eat the restaurant food with her even if you would have preferred your fufu.

Invest on pajamas or romantic shorts or boxers. Your father worn wrapper tied around his waist back them in Nigeria and you still want to wear the same in this 21st century?

Women hate men that are predictable, boring, and not spontaneous.

Do something new. Enroll in a gym, work on your stomach, cut down on beer, to mention but a few.

Allow her to make you feel young and sexy again.

Date her even though you are married. Test each others' boundaries.

Invest in sexy clothes for her to rekindle your youthful days.

Out of intimacy grows love. Offer her the best opportunity to continue to stay in love with you.

In a situation where sexual drive or libido is decreased, due to age or a medical condition, seek medical help to improve your sex life.

Explore other means of satisfying your partner, sexually, no matter how immature it makes you look.

Invest in R-rated movies to spice up your sexual life.

Be spontaneous and avoid the boredom that pushes women away.

Once in awhile, engage in activities out of the blue that will wow her.

If you are a workaholic, stop and "smell the roses" with your wife.

If you work long hours to make ends meet, explain that to your spouse. She will understand. However, if working sixteen hours a day is because you want to live like the Okeres, Okonkwos, or you are investing in a project in Nigeria to impress others, you may ruin your marriage and possibly, your children's lives.

Openly express your love to your wife.

Make her understand why you went for her rather than a woman of your age.

Make her feel good about herself and respect her.

DO NOT control her. She is your wife, irrespective of your age differences.

Never try to change her or expect her to act your age because she is not. Accept love given by her irrespective of her age.

Women

Understand that marriage is for better or for worse.

Remember why you got into the relationship – you love him right?

It is alright to go to the movies alone because he would rather stay home and watch his favorite eighties shows.

Explore his fantasies and treat him to them.

Remember he has been a single man for a while; take it one step at a time.

Do not resent him because he is old fashioned. He did not force you to marry him, you married him willingly.

Seeking intimacy or closeness outside your marriage can be devastating. Maintain an open and honest relationship with your spouse and discuss with him any concerns you make have.

Invite him to activities that can enhance your marital life.

Look out for weekend getaways for couples and attend one with him.

If he enjoys attending conventions, go with him, and spend most of the convention time with him alone in the hotel room.

Get to know your husband more and better.

Chapter 8

Raising an Igbo Child in the Diaspora

by: Stella Nwokeji

A LOST GENERATION?
RAISING AN IGBO CHILD IN THE DIASPORA

In the Diaspora, Igbo parents are faced with a lack of an enabling environment to raise their children according to their accustomed Igbo culture. Children tend to internalise what they see in their environment. Incidentally, Igbo children are exposed to two environments, simultaneously. These are the Igbo environment that they witness at home and the American culture they are exposed to at school and in other activities. Some Igbo kids hardly understand the Igbo language. Some understand it but cannot speak it, while the majority do not understand or speak it. This problem is attributed to parents who introduce English Language, first, to Igbo children in an effort to make them sound "smart". This is not the case when you look at Asian and Hispanic children. Depriving our children the right to learn our Igbo language deprives them also the right to know our Igbo culture. Research studies have shown that children can learn any language at a very early age and also that children who are bilingual are more able to integrate in any new environment or culture. Research also found out that they are more likely to succeed academically. In the midst of the cultural difference, our children are struggling to separate the confusing parenting by their Igbo parents who should know better and those manners they pick up from interacting with others. Our Igbo belief is that it takes a village to raise a child. Collective effort will serve every parent well in raising an Igbo child in the Diaspora. Our children are our investment, which yields dividend if managed well. In accordance with this belief, this chapter illustrates, with a vignette, the challenges encountered by Igbo parents in raising their children in the United States. It also emphasizes suggested solutions to this problem.

Ebube and Udo are the proud parents of Odili, Chychy, Ada, Emeka and Chima. Odili is their first son. He is an 11th grader who loves to play soccer and basketball. He has remained on the Principal's Honor Roll List since he first started grade school. Ada is the first daughter. She is a 10th grader who is an avid volunteer. She has won numerous awards because of her great number of volunteer hours. Chychy is the third daughter of the couple. Chychy is an 8th grader. She loves to read and write. She has had several of her poems and short stories published. Emeka is the second to last son of the couple. Emeka is a 7th grader. He loves to play outside and read as well. Chima is the last daughter and child. She is a 6th grader who loves collecting rocks.

Ebube and Udo are happily married and also gainfully employed. This family is a good example of a typical Igbo family in their community. However, Ebube and Udo always have conflicts about their children because they differ in their child rearing approaches. Ebube, as a father, provides their children with all they ask for, even if it is detrimental to their wellbeing. Udo, on the other hand, believes in "not sparing the rod". She tends to curtail her kids' exposure to the finer things in life. She takes her time to make sure that her three daughters understand their roles as females in Igbo culture. She helps them deal with the gender role prescribed by the Igbo culture, which means that sometimes they are excused from

92

certain activities until the house is cleaned or the meal is prepared. She also tries to inculcate the same habits in the boys who now know how to prepare simple Igbo dishes. Unfortunately, Ebube does not see these responsibilities as necessary. According to him, the girls are born in the United States and are not expected to be raised as typical Igbo women. Moreover, the possibility of their marrying a typical Igbo man is rare.

The couple also has conflicts on the kids' academic responsibilities. While Ebube does not make a conscientious effort to make sure the kids understand the importance of education, Udo takes her time to educate the children on the need to do well, academically. She makes sure that all the kids' assignments and projects are done and turned in on time. Udo is also against the kids having boyfriends or girlfriends or even dating before attending college. This is contrary to Ebube's belief that the kids should have friends and date, as long as they are doing well academically. Ebube has been heard asking the girls about their opposite gender friends and how their relationship is evolving. These conflicts are causing a happy and devoted couple serious marital problems.

SUGGESTIONS FOR PARENTS

General advice:

PRAY, often, as a family for God's guidance in raising your children.

There's no doubt that our Igbo culture does not allow parents to engage in the hugging, kissing and other outward show of affections that the American culture does. However, it is your responsibility to show love to your children as much as possible in the same way that they witness it from their friends' parents.

You are the parents. Pay particular attention to your children. LISTEN TO THEM. They have feelings, too. Listen to what they have to say before you make the final decision on important issues affecting them.

As your children grow, make it a habit to call family meetings to discuss the family's well-being. Call a meeting for every situation, bad or good. Sometimes, allow the children to moderate it and listen to what they have to say.

Take your time to educate your children on your values and what you expect from them.

Make it a point to stress to your children that upholding the family name in a positive light is required of them.

Do not play "god" to your children. Give them the atmosphere to feel free to come to you and discuss issues with you.

As a parent, show them respect and have them show it to you.

Be a role model and lead by example. It is amazing how kids emulate their parents for good or bad. The most effective way to pass on parenting skills to children is by showing by example, rather than teaching them.

Cultivate the idea of "tough love". Use it when possible to maintain boundaries when things are not turning out the way you expect.

Do not take your children as your best friends.

Child rearing is a joint venture and a challenge that both parents must embark on for successful child rearing outcome.

Never use your children as a weapon to make the other spouse envious or worthless. There should not be a popularity contest between parents because child rearing is a joint effort.

Never make the mistake of giving a child everything he or she craves or requests.

Be familiar with the laws of the country you reside in and use them to your benefit. In a situation where spanking or paddling is against the law, use what another method of discipline, such as taking a child's priceless possession as a form of punishment. You can also use the banning method where the child is banned from certain family activities until he or she is on the right page or track. Excluding financial support to a child has been found to be a successful punishment for delinquent children.

Avoid the temptation of having a television set in every room. If they must have the TV, monitor the time they spend on it. Also, set up parental control to avoid exposure to sexually explicit programs.

The same goes to electronic devices. Control the amount of time your child spends on his or her cell phone or ipad. Most cellular phone companies have parental control that can enable you to prevent certain numbers from calling your child or even block the times your child can use his or her number.

Try and teach your children games that the entire family can play and enjoy. Games such as mancala, ludo, chess, checkers, monopoly to mention but a few are great. Playing these games in those days were such bonding time for the family and we enjoyed them growing up. Your kids will too. Have a game night with your kids at least once a week and you will surprise on how they will open up about school, their friends, their fears, etc.

If you're privileged, do not let that affect your children's attitudes and behaviors. Keep all unnecessary luxuries from the children and let them work to earn their own privileges.

Do not be ashamed to correct your child, even when he or she opposes. Every Igbo parent went through the teenage years and survived. If you allow your child to control you, it means he or she has taken over your role as a parent.

Understand that you were brought up in Nigeria and now you are raising your child in America. Let your child rearing skills reflect the best in these different environments.

Make scarifies for your children and let them understand why you are making them.

If possible, cut down on the number of hours you spend at work or meetings, to spend time with your children. Take your children to your Igbo meetings and have them pay attention to what is discussed or deliberated upon.

Go on vacations with your kids. Take them out on spring break or Christmas holiday, to mention but a few. Plan your time and take them to Nigeria at least every two or three years and make sure you have it planned so well that they will have memorable experience. If you can afford it, explore other places such as Europe to give them the exposure that academics only cannot give them.

Taking your kids on vacation where you stay with family members is not a vacation because the kids end up staying indoors while the adults cruise around the city. Vacation should be a time for you to bond with your kids and wife. However, in the process, you can visit a relative or two if time permits.

When you go to a convention, it is okay to make it a family vacation. Ttake the children with you and use it as an opportunity to spend time with them. Monitor where they are and never leave them at the hotel lobby while you dance the night away.

If you are called to the high table, make sure you know who will take care of your children while you are there. After taking your seat at the high table, let one of you, probably the wife come down and stay with your children.

Give your children privacy but monitor what they do as children.

Reach out to your community in raising your children. You can learn a lot from what works for other parents.

Academic advice:

A child's academic success starts with a parent making the right decision about their children's academic life and future. Decide early what type of school you want your children to attend – private or public. If you decide on public, make sure you live in a good school district, in order to give your child the best school experience in which they will excel, academically.

If you can afford it, have one parent stay at home after school when the children need guidance for home work and extracurricular activities.

Start early to give your kids the best weapon for success. Encourage them to READ, READ, and READ. Let them read anything in order to cultivate their habit of reading.

Let your child know, at the onset, that grades matter, contrary to what may be obtainable in their friends' homes.

Use the opportunity to let them know that going to a university is not an option but an expectation and help them work towards that compulsory goal.

Be your child's first guidance counselor at home. Start planning early for your kids' academic lives. Guide them and go with him or her to see the school guidance counselor.

Schools and teachers like to see parents who are involved and committed. Let them know that you care about your kids' academic success. Visit your child's teacher, ask questions, and call the teacher when your child is not doing well to ascertain the reason and know how to help him or her.

Chaperon during your child's school field trips and get to know his or her teachers and friends.

Attend the Parents Teachers Association meetings and get involved. You will be surprised at the amount of information you can get to help your child succeed.

Get your kids involved in extracurricular activities and be there to take them to the events. Support them. Chose an activity your child is interested in and also that is recognized by college recruiters. Make sure that they join clubs in their schools. Pay attention to the clubs that pertain to what they actually want to do in life. An example will be joining the Science Olympiad Club (science inclined child) or Mock Trial (liberal arts inclined child).

Church activities are also extracurricular activities. Get them involved spiritually and nurture that.

Middle school is the most important time in your child's life. Make the effort to understand where your child is, academically. Show him or her that you care. No matter how busy you are, take the time to ask them simple question on how they did in school that day.

If you have the time, teach your children. Help them understand the concept taught in school or teach them how to get ahead of their course work.

If your child is struggling, get a paid tutor to help your child. Your child is your priced possession. Invest in him or her.

Get to know your child's friends and make sure they guide him or her to make good choices.

Help your child succeed. Show them and their teachers that you care.

Encourage the teachers to feel free to contact you, whenever possible, to discuss your child's successes or failures.

Teach your children to be at their best behavior each time he or she is at school. Teachers tend to cling more to those students who are well disciplined and academically sound.

If you notice that a particular teacher is not a good fit for your child, you have the right to request a conference and discuss that with your child's teacher. If you do not see any improvement, go through the next chain of command until you get an answer or a solution to the problem.

If your child rides the school bus to school, make an effort to be there to send or pick up him or her. However, on your off days, take the extra step and pick or drop your child from school. This period will provide a wonderful opportunity to interact with your children.

BE PROACTIVE AND BE YOUR CHILD'S ADVOCATE!

In conclusion, marital relationship is a complex process which is both ceremonious and lengthy. Both men and women get into marriage for different reasons. With the advancement of education, Igbo women are getting empowered more than ever to compete in the society they find themselves in. Today, Igbo men are marrying because of the opportunity education is bringing to Igbo women, however, some of these men still hang on to our traditional Igbo culture of male supremacy. Similarly, Igbo men are spending more time acquiring higher education that they are in their forties when they start making arrangements for marriage. In a mutual relationship where both individuals understand each other, age is not an issue. Igbo men deserve respect irrespective of which society we are in or who is making the most money in the family. The saying in Igboland that the pride of a woman is her husband still holds today, if we take out the male chauvinistic attitude. I strongly believe that a man complements and completes a woman and vice versa

As much as we expect Igbo wives to live up to the Igbo traditional marriage culture, we cannot be naive to the fact that western education and exposure has liberated women. Some male chauvinistic behaviors toward marriage should be curtailed. Please note that I am not advocating for elimination of our Igbo marriage culture. Instead, I am of the opinion that we must adjust according to the ever changing world. As a global village, our way of life should reflect these changes. Igbo marriage culture should not be an exception. We must accept and accommodate the evolving global marital life to avoid disaster.

Chapter 9

The Americanized Igbo Marriage

by: Rev. Sunday Eke-Okoro

Spiritual Application of Culture

Marriage is a complex process that cannot be successfully handled by human effort. Marriage requires a Trinitarian image to be realistic. The Trinitarian image involves the presence of the divine in the union of husband and wife. Divine presence calls for the recognition of the fact that culture of origin of spouses is divinely and specifically characterized in such a way that ignoring the essentials of such culture is usually counterproductive. To reject your God-given culture for a foreign culture in order to belong is never helpful in marriage. It is true that laws and regulations of alien culture may create the impression of fairness to spouses. However, the applications of such laws and regulations to persons of different cultural origin may not have a good fit, especially if spirituality is ignored. How could foreign cultures help marriages, since they are usually at variance with original culture into which one is born? Here again, it will be noted that international and interracial marriages are becoming significant and usually bring about a clash of cultures. Help may come from multiple cultures if they are tied to Christian spirituality. Spirituality brings all things to an operational unity. No matter the type of marriage one is involved with, marriage is a process that is spiritually designed for success. For instance love, procreation and security are special gifts of God that prime spousal union for success. Germane to this fact is that "He who finds a wife finds what is good and receives favor from the LORD." (Proverbs 18:22).

In previous works on marriage and family1 (Eke-Okoro 2002, 2005), it has been shown that marriage is not a bed of roses, but a ministry field in which you have to work on before it can succeed. Igbos in the United States have no excuses for allowing their marriages to fail. The Igbo people are well known for their strong marital values and marriage breakdown is usually a shameful thing. That is why a lot of groundwork is usually done in spousal selection. In fact, it is usually a marriage between the two families of the couple. Interestingly, the strong Christian values of the Igbos have been a very helpful input in marriage and families such that spouses are always there for each other and their children. The mutual respect between husband and wife in Igbo marriage could not be replaced by the fact that a spouse receives more financial income than the other.

In the Igbo culture and also in Christianity, wife and husband are advised to "submit" to one another out of reverence for Christ. For wives, this means submit to your husbands as to the Lord for a husband is the head of his wife as Christ is the head of the Church. He is the Savior of his body, the Church. As the Church submits to Christ, so you wives should submit to your husbands in everything. For husbands, this means love your wives, just as Christ loved the Church. He gave up his life for her to make her holy and clean, washed by the cleansing of God's word. He did this to present her to himself as a glorious Church without a spot or wrinkle or any other blemish. Instead, she will be holy and without fault. In the same way, husbands ought to love their wives as they love their own bodies. For a man who loves his wife actually shows love for himself. No one hates his own body but feeds and cares for it, just as Christ cares for the church." (Ephesians 5:21-29 NLT).

CAUSES OF MARITAL DISRUPTION

Financial Inequality

It has been claimed that financial inequality among spouses is one of the sources of disrespect in Igbo marriage in the Diaspora. Remember that "the love of money is a root of all kinds of evil. Some people, eager for money, have wandered from the faith and pierced themselves with grief." (1Timothy 6:10).   Disrespect related to unequal financial income has been significantly identified as coming from a higher income wife. This should not be the case at all if the wife understands that her income is a gift from God for their family. If a husband should not look down on his wife because of his higher financial income, why should a wife disrespect her husband because of her higher income? A wife who does so must recognize that disrespecting her husband is counterproductive, because the two spouses are one person in marriage: "No one hates his/her own body but feeds and cares for it, just as Christ cares for the church. And we are members of his body. As the Scriptures say, 'A man leaves his father and mother and is joined to his wife, and the two are united into one.' This is a great mystery, but it is an illustration of the way Christ and the Church are one. So again I say, each man must love his wife as he loves himself, and the wife must respect her husband." (Ephesians 5:29-33).

Improper Selection of Spouse

The spirituality of marriage is related to a proper selection of spouse. It has been remarked that in the Igbo culture, marriage is not just between the two partner spouses, but also between the two families of origin of the spouses. The role of the families of origin of the spouses in enduring marital relationship cannot be overemphasized. In the Igbo tradition, there must be a proper illumination of the persons and families of origin of spouses going into a marital union. There cannot be a mistake in doing this, unless one is ready to invest in trouble after marriage. This is consistent with the Christian approach to marriage: "Don't team up with those who are unbelievers." How can righteousness be a partner with wickedness? How can light live with darkness? What harmony can there be between Christ and the devil? How can a believer be a partner with an unbeliever? And what union can there be between God's temple and idols? For we are the temple of the living God. As God said: "I will live in them and walk among them. I will be their God, and they will be my people. Therefore, come out from among unbelievers, and separate yourselves from them, says the Lord. Don't touch their filthy things, and I will welcome you. And I will be your Father, and you will be my sons and daughters, says the Lord Almighty." (2 Corinthians 6:14-18). A family of origin known for robbery or other criminal activities would disqualify their child from marriage with a person from a more respectable and honorable family. Again in the Igbo practice of marriage, despite a similar culture, marriage may not be possible if a partner is not a practicing Christian.

The implication of the Christian connection is the promise of God to be part of the marital union. Without God being in a marriage, there will be no true love because God is Love. God has promised to live among the spouses and walk among them. God will be their God, and they will be God's people. Therefore, as a guarantee of God's role in your marriage, you must not get married with any person who has not accepted Jesus Christ as Lord and personal Savior. Come out from any plans of getting into marriage partnership with an unbeliever. Don't touch the filthy things the unbelievers do, and God will welcome you, lead you to the right partner and also be part of your marriage.

The Hanging-Out Factor

"Do not be misled: Bad company corrupts good character. Come back to your senses as you ought, and stop sinning; for there are some who are ignorant of God—I say this to your shame." (1 Corinthians 15:33-34). You cannot be hanging out with people who teach you things that will destroy your marriage. Remember that the whole purpose of Satan is to destroy your marriage. Satan will use your job colleagues who you hang out with during your break period to destroy your marriage. When you get back home they continue their diabolic plans on phone, and they would not stop until they have caused havoc in your marriage. They will advise you to be in control because your income is greater than that of your spouse. They will lead you into immoral sexual activities against your spouse. In fact, they will shamelessly drive you into senseless selfish activities in order to steal, kill and destroy your marriage and family. You cannot be listening to that rubbish without causing a mess in your marriage and family. Get out of them and be separate. Bad company corrupts good moral character. When they destroy your marriage, they will be the first to backbite you negatively. After destroying you, they leave you to suffer the consequences alone. Please, come to your senses and save your marriage from satanic disruption.

You should also stop engaging in unnecessary comparisons. Marriages differ in various ways. All you need to do is to prayerfully work on your marriage for success and endurance. Comparison of the possessions of other families or individuals is also dangerous and could lead to unhelpful expenditures that could put the finances of your family in a bad shape. Spouses should always discuss their financial state and determine what is best for them.

Children

Spousal role in the socialization of their children could create marital problems or be a blessing for the family. Children should be trained in such a way that they bring honor to the family and society. There has been evidence that some Igbo families in their infatuation with the American experience fail to discipline their children. When attention is drawn to that fact, they claim "umu America" (they are American Children) as an excuse for not doing their work in training their children appropriately. The "umu America" (they are American Children) excuse is not be acceptable. It is simply a destruction of those kids and a repudiation of the Christianized Igbo culture. That's a shame! Start your children off on the way they should go, and even when they are old they will not turn from it. Do not withhold discipline from a child; if you punish your children with the rod, they will not die. Punish them with the rod and save them from death. (Proverbs 22:6, 23:13, 14). If you refuse to discipline your child, he/she can harm you, physically and emotionally. Do not lose your God-given children because of a lack of discipline. Start early or it would be too late to do anything effective.

Single parenthood is never good for children when it can be avoided. Children need both mother and father in the home. You should not deny them that privilege. Single parenthood has been a disaster everywhere and should never be generated by any spouse. Children need role models and as such, parents should conduct themselves honorably in the presence of their children. You husband and you wife, "Drink water from your own cistern, running water from your own well. Should your springs overflow in the streets, your streams of water in the public squares? Let them be yours alone, never to be shared with strangers. May your fountain be blessed, and may you rejoice in the wife/husband of your youth. A loving doe, a graceful deer—may her breasts/his masculinity satisfy you always, may you ever be intoxicated with her/his love. Why, my son/daughter, be intoxicated with another man's wife/husband? Why embrace the bosom of a wayward woman/man?" (Proverbs 5:15). Immorality, more than anything else, would destroy your marriage. You should also not blackmail or disgrace or even belittle your spouse in the presence of your child/children/outsiders. It is a foolish act that is usually counterproductive.

Spousal Parents & Spousal Siblings

It has been earlier remarked that Igbo marriage is not only between spouses but also between spousal families of origin. This pattern has merits and demerits in relation to the emerging family of the spouses. It is important for spouses to know that while they respect and honor their respective parents and siblings, care must be taken to avoid their taking control of events in your emerging family. Your spouse must have the first place in your marriage before any member of your family of origin. Your spouse is yourself and yourself is your spouse because two of you are one in marriage. When any member of spousal family visits, you must give him/her good hospitality, but he/she must not dictate for you how you and your spouse should run the affairs of your marriage and family. You may listen to their advice in troubling marital situations, but their advice should only be taken as a suggestion that may be adopted or rejected. They are only visitors in your home, not controllers of affairs in your family. You should be careful because some of them could turn out to be selfish dictators who can destroy your marriage. Their dictates may be related to what they hope to gain from isolating a spouse who they consider an obstacle to their selfish end.

The only person who is allowed to be in a total control of the affairs of your family is the Almighty God who made your marriage possible. "Commit to the LORD whatever you do, and he will establish your plans." (Proverbs 16:3). After all, God said, "He who finds a wife finds what is good and receives favor from the LORD." (Proverbs 18:22). Divine favor is your portion if you allow God to be in charge of your marriage and family. Joshua said, "As for me and my household, we will serve the LORD." (Joshua 24:15b). That was an impressive and victory statement by Joshua about his marriage and family. God loved Joshua and he further advised Joshua: "Keep this Book of the Law always on your lips; meditate on it day and night, so that you may be careful to do everything written in it. Then you will be prosperous and successful." (Joshua 1:8). Joshua had an excellent family and he never messed up. What are you waiting for? Does your family serve the Lord and worship him together in morning and evening prayers, in the dining table, in family fasting, in daily Bible reading, and in meaningful Church membership? Who is going to start it for you if you don't? Remember that if you ignore God, you are investing in trouble in your marriage and family.

(Endnotes)

1   Eke-Okoro, ST. (2002). Family Love & Spousal Equity. Dorrance Publishing Co. Pittsburgh PA.

Eke-Okoro, ST. (2005). Marriage & Family Enrichment Bible Studies. Holy Fire Publishing, Martinsburg, WV.

Scripture References are from the New International Version

Chapter 10

The Untouchables

by: Azubike Aliche

I write this, essentially, for my fellow men and husbands, particularly those who believe firmly in orthodox gender relations. If you physically or emotionally abuse your wife or seek to control her every move, I urge you to think again before continuing. It is potentially dangerous for you! If you take for granted that your wife will always play subordinate role in your house, you are in for a rude shock. Chances are that when your wife arrived here in the United States, she appeared docile, domesticated and was unquestionably willing to submit to your authority. Have you wondered why she now argues with you and dares you to do your worse? I'll attempt to address that issue. My take is that the culture here, that is the environment, is responsible!

When the Igbo wife arrives the shores of the United States and into the warm, welcoming arms of her husband, she is definitely vulnerable to abuse and exploitation. However, if you look closely you will find that she comes with what it takes to live independently, if the marriage turns out to be something other than what she wants. The things that make her vulnerable include the fact that she, most probably, came with your immigration sponsorship, would not have a job in the first few months, at least, and would not know the roads and other geographical attributes of her new city of residence. Other factors include the fact that she may not have relatives here and, possibly, may have difficulty understanding American English or accent. However, when you balance these challenges with the resources that she brings, and the legal protections guaranteed her by the American government and society, you find the ingredients that will enable her to rebel, if she chooses to.

After speaking with many of you, in the course of gathering materials for this book, I now know that many of the problems that plague some Igbo marriages in the United States do not start in the first year of the marriage. They start when your wife has had her legal status sorted out, when she has got a job and, sometimes, making more money than you. Marital problems have arisen when you've had a child or two together, when she's known about the laws on domestic violence and services available to victims of domestic violence and when she has made friends here and known how to spend hours on the phone with other women, Nigerian or American. Many of you have told me that what irks you the most and spark trouble is when your wife begins to question what you believe to be your traditional authority, as head of the family.

When you think of the resources that our wives bring with them into this country, education comes to mind, easily. Many of our wives arrive here more educated than their sponsoring husbands. More importantly, many arrive with skills that are in high demand, such as nurses. One result of this is that many of these wives get a job soon after they arrive since, in most cases, they come in as permanent residents. Unlike their husbands, some of who spent years chasing the all important Green Card, these women are able to join the labor force and make good money and other health benefits shortly after arriving here. Some end up making more money than their husbands, in record time. Others become the sole breadwinner in the family. Once a woman begins to contribute a significant portion of the family income, the tendency is that she wants a bigger share on how that money is spent and other decision points in the household. Trouble begins when she's denied this. In reaction, she can open her own bank account and release only what she wants to contribute to the family, if at all. And, depending on who the husband is, he may see this as a challenge to his authority, as the traditional head of the family. And so begins trouble.

Related to education and occupation is language. Compared with a woman from across the border in Mexico who enters the United State not knowing how to speak English, the Igbo wife has the advantage of arriving from thousands of miles fluent in the English language. Thanks to the fact that Nigeria and the US share a common history of colonial rule by Great Britain. The economic difficulties that Nigeria has had to go through in the better part of the last 30 years has made Nigerian men living abroad as the most sought after suitors. They are able to beat the competition for the best educated girls in Nigeria. Young women, anywhere in the world, like a good life that the American society can offer. Besides, they want social security for themselves and their future children. Life in the industrialized countries, such as United States, Canada, and Britain are especially attractive because of the high standard of living and the fact that English is the main language of communication. When our wives arrive here, they are basically ready for the job market or the schools, without worrying about learning a foreign language. The most that they could be required to study before they are offered employment or school admission is English as a Second Language (ESL). In many cases, because they are young and more adaptable, they are better able to speak in more accessible accent than their older husbands who did not grow up in the age of the television in Nigeria.

The ability to speak the English language becomes very valuable to our wives in the sense that they can more easily adapt to the host culture, including learning the laws, legal system and the services available to abused immigrant wives. So, their language skills open the gate to many other opportunities for personal advancement and possible independent living. The more our wives gain greater knowledge about the structures and institutions of the host country and how these guarantee their rights and freedoms, the greater the chance of trouble for an abusive and controlling husband. Such wives are better prepared to challenge some of the traditional gender roles that appear unfair to women and this challenge is often interpreted to mean a challenge on her husband's authority and manhood. When this happens, the delicate balance of power in the home is disturbed and the stage is set for conflict.

The other thing to consider is that the more our wives stay in the United States, the more they expand their formal and informal social networks, something that virtually heals the initial sense of isolation that many of them feel upon arrival in this foreign land. Only a few short years ago, virtually only the phone (land line) was available to them, and then the cell phones. Today, the popular social networks, particularly Facebook, have come into the mix, not to leave out the ubiquitous handheld devises that enable use of email and texting. At the workplace and even in informal meetings or ceremonies, women have further opportunities to share information with others of their kind and to compare notes on how their marriages are going. I know of some Igbo men who have attempted to control how often their wives can use the phone or communicate with other women, particularly American women. I know too that they have succeeded only for a short time until their wives realize their rights and what bargaining power they have by making some of most of the money from which the phone bill is paid. It's even more difficult today when cell phones have become ubiquitous and can be picked up for free, depending on what payment plan you want.

In discussing the sources of power for our wives, it is important to consider that there were a number of landmark legislations and social movements in the mid 1990s that had the effect of guaranteeing women protection from abuse of their human rights and freedoms. A consequence of these is that our wives have safety nets available for them, should they get into trouble with their dominating husbands when they ask for more equitable relationship at home. In 1994, here in the United States, the landmark Violence Against Women Act was enacted. For the first time, Congress took bold steps to protect immigrant women, including those of them living illegally in the country, through that piece of legislation. It had provisions that could enable a woman who is a victim of domestic violence to obtain legal residence on her own, given certain conditions stipulated in that legislation. On December 7, 2000, the Violence Against Women Act was amended to give immigrant women even more protection from domestic violence. The amendment allowed undocumented women to file to cancel deportation proceedings if their case is pending. Under the amended legislation, women were no longer required to show proof of extreme hardship, as condition to file for permanent residence. In fact, the amendment allowed women to petition based on abuse that took place outside the United States. Further aid to immigrant women dealing with domestic violence came when the then Immigration and Naturalization Service (INS) and the US Department of Justice issued proposals that allowed victims of domestic violence to be one of only five protected groups to apply for asylum. The other protected groups are people seeking asylum because they were being persecuted based on their political opinion, nationality, race and religion. What that means is that an illegal alien woman can file for asylum in the United States just by showing evidence that she's a victim of domestic violence. That way, her husband is not able to oppress her because he brought her here, undocumented, or that he filed for permanent residence for her.

Another monumental event that helped the cause of women living with domestic violence and other forms of oppression by men came the following year, in far away Beijing China. It is the United Nations Fourth World Conference on Women, held in September 1995. That conference raised awareness about the rights of women, worldwide. One outcome of that conference is the issuance of the Declaration on the Elimination of all forms of Discrimination Against Women. In particular, that conference produced a Declaration on the Elimination of Violence Against Women and, effectively, made violence against women a violation of their human rights.

The Danger Zone

Men who have difficulty changing the beliefs about marriage and gender roles that they brought from Igbo land are more likely to enter what I'll call a danger zone in their marriages, particularly if their wives don't share those beliefs. Each time I remember Ekaette, my deputy many years ago when I work in a newspaper house in Port Harcourt, I remember how she used to classify her roles outside the work place into "wifely" and "mothering" roles. We used to laugh about it but nothing illustrates our traditional expectation of our wives than that. We think in terms of what roles that culture and society has prescribed for men and women and only few of us are able to transcend that. In plain language, what I'm saying is that we, Igbo men, come to the industrialized Western countries with our socio-cultural ideology intact. Incidentally, that ideology reserves a lesser status for women and leaves them with a disproportionate share of household duties. They were expected to serve the man, among other responsibilities! And it sets the stage for what may be our relationship with our wives, unless we understand that culture is dynamic, rather than static.

It is unrealistic to expect that, in relating with our wives, nothing about our cultural values and beliefs will intervene or interject. They do play a role on our attitude towards how we view what they say to us and how they say it, how they manage the money they earn, who becomes their friends, whether they cook, and what they cook, how much they are available for their "wifely" obligations, and even what they wear, etc. Ordinarily, the more a man is flexible and adaptable in his cultural values and beliefs, the more he's able to live in peace with his wife, given the environmental factors at play here. But some men have told me that they consider themselves duty bound to preserve Igbo culture and values and that the way they relate to their wives will determine what they pass on to their sons for the next generation. I can understand that but caution is warranted and walking a fine line between keeping pristine values and according your wife respect for her rights is recommended to save your marriage. The more pragmatic people are in dealing with everyday events in their relationship, the better.

I do not give the impression that Igbo wives are not interested in upholding Igbo cultural values and beliefs or that upholding these beliefs and expressing them in marriage are necessarily incompatible with a peaceful relationship. If partners in marriage share these values and make them a part of their lives, peace will prevail. What many women have told me is that there are stressors arising from living in this foreign land and other work and social commitments that make any adherence to orthodox Igbo socio-cultural and gender ideologies impracticable or prone to friction. Let us consider, for example, our nurse-wives. I choose this group because, from media reports, this group is at higher risk than any other group to be victims of domestic violence, most probably because they experience a lot of these stressors while making a lot of money, particularly when they work over time. Many of our nurse wives work night duty and hardly regain lost sleep during the day. Many of them work more than one job at a time or work more than one shift. Many of them have more than two children to take care of. Some of them are in school, part time or full time. In the work place, some are dealing with discrimination, sometimes because of their color of skin or manner of speaking. Without holding brief for our nurse-wives, it is reasonable to assume that they will have to spend so much time and energy outside the home that they would be too exhausted when they return, to be able to fulfill their "wifely" and "mothering" roles. That is where a husband who is not rigid in his attitude to traditional gender roles comes in. Whether it is chores, sex, or childcare, the husband here can be more realistic in his expectations of his wife, despite what the orthodox gender roles prescribe.

What we find and which is a source of problem is that the more the economic status of women change for the better, because they grow in their jobs and make more money, the more at risk of domestic violence they become, particularly if they earn more than their husbands and assert their authority over this money or how it should be spent. This is something that both Igbo men and women should pay attention to and plan ahead for, even before they marry. It doesn't hurt to have prenuptial agreement on how family incomes should be controlled and spent, including questions about whether the partners should have joint and individual bank accounts and how immediate relatives should be given money. As stated earlier, Igbo sociocultural ideology prescribes a subordinate status for the wife, vis-à-vis her husband. The expectation is that a man owns whatever his wife brings into the family. The problem is that in Igbo land, few women really bring anything substantial or more than the husband into the marriage. So, traditional gender relations is put in jeopardy once, as is the case in industrialized countries, a women has higher economic power than her husband, as this has implications for power dynamics in the family. Experience has shown that it's easier to ask a woman to bring herself and everything she earns under the authority of her husband than it is realistic. The legal protections that our women have, here, have made it even more unrealistic an expectation. Some men who, whether in allegiance to Igbo customs or otherwise, have ignored the laws and resorted to intimate partner violence to enforce their perceived authority have had to pay a huge price, in the form of long jail terms, payment of fines and more.

The challenge before Igbo couples is to work out how the wife's status in the family can improve as her economic status improves. That is the recipe for peace and family cohesion. After all, in Igbo land, men acquired their higher status over women because, by tradition, they owned/inherited family property and other means of production. In many cases, boys were sent to school at the expense of girls, if the family did not have enough resources to train both, because we have a patrilineal (patriarchal) system in Igbo land. In the developed countries, such as the United States, achievement, rather than ascription, is the source of social status.

But, even with improved economic status, Igbo women still owe a duty to walk a fine line in their relationship with their husbands to ensure that a man's authority is preserved in the home. She does this by according her husband the necessary courtesies and respect. Some Igbo men who are not beholden by traditional gender structures have told me that their concern is that their wives do not allow them to profit from their monetary investments in bringing the women over here and in training them or even in taking care of the home while the women worked or schooled. I hope that our women pay attention to this group, as playing winner-takes-all can be a source of conflict, legitimately perhaps. What is needed is effective communication in the family. Nobody says that a good marriage is one that has no problems. No. The hallmark of a good marriage is one in which the parties work through their problems, by talking about it and resolving the issues that cause problem in the marriage. In a good marriage, there is no room for power struggles, as these tend to leave resentment on their paths. When each partner digs in and sticks out his or her ego, nothing is resolved. The problem with good marriages is not the occasional arguments but what the parties do after to repair any ill feelings following the arguments. Emotional intelligence and regulation are important assets that couples can bring to their marriage, if they want to be happy in it and stay longer. Healthy communication skills, conflict resolutions skills and problem solving skills are needed to navigate through the cultural prescriptions in our heads going into the marriage and harmonize them with the demands of living in a foreign industrialized land with all the stressors that come with it.

The Risk

Domestic violence has serious consequences for the victim, man or woman. On the other hand, it has great risks for the perpetrator, including risk of imprisonment, particularly here in the United States. Whoever first reports a case of domestic violence is usually considered the plaintiff. For the defendant, the immediate consequence is a restraining order imposed by the courts. Under the Prevention of Domestic Violence Act of the State of New Jersey, a defendant can face the following punishments and other legal sanctions:

- Prohibition against future acts of domestic violence.
- Prohibition from living in the house he shared with the plaintiff or wherever the plaintiff lives or even from visiting something like a school where his child attends.
- Prohibition from having any kind of contact/communication with the plaintiff – oral, written, personal, electronic, etc. – or even of one's child or children.
- Prohibition from making or causing anyone to make harassing communication to the plaintiff or someone else, including one's children.
- Prohibition from stalking, following, or threatening harm to the plaintiff or someone else.
- Monetary payment to the plaintiff in emergency monetary relief or to care for a dependent.
- Requirement to attend a substance abuse, mental health or other evaluations and/or treatment programs.

111

- Order to go submit to psychiatric evaluation.
- Prohibition from possessing weapons or firearms and/or to surrender such weapons or firearms and the license to possess them

On the other hand, the plaintiff can be awarded the house that he or she lived with the defendant. Also, the plaintiff can be awarded sole custody of the couple's children.

There are good reasons to believe that an Igbo woman living in an abusive marriage may not report it to authorities. This is because, in Igbo culture, an Igbo woman would live in silence with domestic violence but no one should stretch this too far. Back home, reporting domestic relations problems to the police is rare, not so much because the domestic violence laws are weak and the police may be nonchalant or even complicit. It has to do with the social norm in which such disputes are settled within the larger extended family on both sides of the family or even through the intervention of trusted friends. That tradition has survived to a lesser extent here in the Diaspora. In fact, some of the Igbo wives killed here in the US by their husbands may have lived if they had reported the violence on time. What happens is that the typical Igbo woman is oriented to make sacrifices for the interest of other family members, including their husbands. Many women have stayed in abusive relationships in the interest of their children. Also, by the nature of Igbo culture and how we are raised, we tend to discourage divorce at any cost and a woman who leaves her husband is almost always ostracized.

I know a woman who divorced her husband a few years ago and other Igbo women were telling her that her female children may not find suitors because of a perception that they, just like their mother, cannot stand marriage nor do what it takes to remain in marriage. Invariably, Igbo women are often blamed for a failed marriage and some do even see it as a personal failure if their marriage failed. In many cases, many Igbo women treat their relationship with their husbands as intimate, such that it is not something that they want to make a public matter, which could be the case, if a court case arises. Such women tend to have a sense of shame if their marriage fails or the problems they are having in it becomes a public matter. Related to that is what is considered the image of the family or even the ethnic group that has to be protected. Also, it's not in our culture to live in shelter, have children temporarily removed from the home or to suffer other inconveniences that can result when domestic violence is reported to the authorities. Again, no man should take for granted that his abused spouse will remain silent forever.

If it looks like the focus here is on men, as perpetrators, it is because of the patriarchal ideologies that is infused in Igbo culture and the fact that a 1999 study showed that, in the United States, "up to 95 percent of all domestic violence cases between adults are of violence against women." Also, while up to 10 Igbo men have reportedly killed their wives in the United States in the last decade, there is hardly any report of an Igbo woman who killed her husband.

Advice from my friends, examples from my parents

When I wedded in October 2001, in Nigeria, my friend, Tunde Ipinmisho, came hundreds of miles from Abuja to support. Gabriel Onwuka came from Aba, about 25 miles away. They were not the only guests but they stand out, in terms of what they said at the occasion. Tunde told me how the first five years of marriage was critical for the future of the relationship. He noted that this was a turbulent period for any marriage, as the partners struggle to bond. Dee Gab, as we fondly called him in school, compared women to ripe tomatoes. He told me that husbands handle their wives (like ripe tomatoes) with care or break the relationship. These had been married many years and were sharing life experiences. On my return to the US, Anthony Egbulefu, another school mate who lives in Chicago, warned me that no man relies on his wife's money, if he wants stability in their marriage. Holding these pieces of advice close to my chest has helped me in the last decade to navigate my own marriage, with all the contours in it. In terms of attitude to gender relations, I give credit to my late mother, Grace Nkechi Aliche, who always reminded her three boys that doing household chores does not damage a boy's genital organs. In other words, you can still do those things traditionally reserved for girls and yet remain a boy. And everyone who knows my late father, Jonah Chiehika Aliche, knows that he was a hands-on dad who would cook, clean or bath us, if mom was not available. It has helped. So, what has socialization got to do with it?

Chapter 11

Thoughts on Marriage

by: Valentine Iwuchukwu

It is necessary to address our thoughts seriously on marriage and family matters and seek to understand them in the right perspective. It is not just looking at the concepts from the angle of what it has become but also from what it ought to be. This is necessary because if marriage is understood in its true significance, those concerned will consciously approach this sacred institution with the right mindset and be able to weather the storm when it eventually comes.

Marriage is the union of two persons of opposite sex in matrimony, to the exclusion of all others. This no doubt is the definition of marriage from the Western/Christian point of view, though conservative because it does not respect polygamy or same sex marriages. Nevertheless, it is good enough definition for our discussion here.

Everything has its rules, which must be followed to achieve good results. These laws are fundamental to the success of every endeavor and they are the natural laws in which the entire creation came into being and exist. The basis of understanding marriage and, indeed, all life and existence lies in the knowledge of Divine Laws of Creation, which is the manifestation of the Will of God. This may be called the Laws of God and they incorporate the Laws of Nature. The laws of nature have always existed and will continue to exist; hence they are called Eternal Laws. They do not change, and cannot be subverted or circumvented. They apply to everyone, irrespective of circumstances, religions and beliefs. The effects of these Laws are the same to those who know them as on those who are ignorant of them. Ignorance is no excuse!

For a deeper understanding of these Laws, let us contrast it with the laws that men make. Secular laws or laws of human beings on earth vary from one society to another. What is lawful in one country may not be lawful in another country. What is perfectly legal yesterday may be changed and may become a criminal act today. The Laws of Creation are the same everywhere. Unlike human laws with its imperfections and dynamic, the natural law is immutable, irrevocable, and inexorable. Natural laws do not call for interpretations of those learned in earthly laws; it is unchangeable.

Human laws are many, complicated and difficult to understand. Therefore, we often depend on lawyers who have devoted years of study to master these secular laws for its interpretation. And, even, lawyers do not always agree on the interpretation of a given law and that is why the idea of a judge is necessary. Judges sometimes differ while interpreting a particular law. No educational programs, in ordinary sense of the expression, are required to interpret the Natural Laws. Human laws do not always promote justice, quite often "smart" lawyers capitalize on legal loopholes to set free people who have actually committed crimes. Some people suffer and sometimes die for crimes they know nothing about. Moreover, some laws are made to serve private and personal interests. In contrast, the Laws of Creation ensure that Justice, Love, and Purity are simultaneously upheld at all times.

Any individual, irrespective of circumstance, that obeys these laws discussed below and apply it to his or her marriage will experience marital bliss. Unlike large number of laws that men make for themselves, the laws under discussion are just three interrelated and complementary Laws. They are:

1 The law of Sowing and Reaping.

2 The law of Attraction of Homogeneous Species and

3 The Law of Spiritual Gravitation

The first is the Law by which God maintains Creation, it is popularly expressed in the words "whatever you sow, you are obliged to reap". This Law is described in other expressions which include the Law of Karma; the Law of Seed and Harvest; the Law of Cause and Effect; the Law of Reciprocal Action; and the Law of Retributive Justice. It is a Law that everyone should be familiar with for its manifestation is everywhere in Creation.

The natural law which is most appropriate for our discussion on this marriage issue is the second law above: The Law of Attraction of Homogeneous Species. This can be seen as the law of like attracts like; Law of Homogeneity; Law of similar Species. The saying "Birds of the same feather flock together" is a variant of this Law. So also is the saying "Show me your friend and I will tell you who you are" or "Show me your husband and I will tell you who you are." Just as birds of the same feather flock together, so do fishes of the same kind congregate. They congregate to move together in large groups called shoals or schools. This congregation put them to advantage; they are driven by collective desire to avoid strong waves and find their food easily. Any of them that strays is most likely to be swept by strong current and the inherent danger of being eaten by a bigger fish or other predators.

The law of Homogeneity manifests itself in the relationships among persons and is also manifest in natural communities of plants and animals. Those who can recall what they studied in elementary chemistry can see the effect of the Law quite clearly. In elementary, chemistry we are taught that identical molecules come together to form compounds, as well as in many chemical reactions. This Law, also, ensures that if particular specie splits, the split parts will unite when the opportunity arises. It is for this reason that opposite poles of a magnet attract.

Let us examine this closely. Stephen M. Lampe in his book The Christian and Reincarnation (Millennium Press, Ibadan Nigeria, 2008) succinctly explained it thus: "Consider a bar magnet. Suppose we hold this magnet in such a way that the left end is the South Pole and the right end is the North Pole. Imagine that we then cut the bar magnet into two (the two parts need to be equal). We now have two bar magnets. Call the left piece "magnet A" and the right piece "magnet B". By convention the right end of "magnet A" is a new north pole, while the left end of "magnet B" becomes a new south pole. But remember that the right end of "magnet A" (the new north pole) and the left end of "magnet B" (the South Pole) were one and the same point before we cut the original bar magnet into two. Therefore when the new North Pole attracts the new South Pole, we are merely witnessing the coming together of closely similar parts that were forcibly separated; adjacent molecules that were separated are given a chance to rejoin.

And they do so in accordance with the Creation Law of "Like Attracts Like." Whole species that are similar will attract. But so will the split parts of the same species seek to reunite."

Thus the law of Attraction of Homogeneous Species is fundamental for everything that is striving for a union in Creation. So follow me calmly and you will soon understand why a thorough understanding and application of this law is an essential knowledge for a successful marriage. Even nation states of similar characteristics will always find common grounds to move ahead together. This is so even in situation where a particular country is forced to split, due to overwhelming circumstances. Such a country will not attain its full potential without reuniting, as we have seen with the reunification of east and west Germany to today's Germany.

The Law of Attraction of Homogeneous Species takes place between whole species that are similar, and the desire of the split parts of the same definite specie. The human being is not a whole species but only a splitting part, which carries the natural desire for union of similar specie. This explains the natural attraction between man and woman.

The natural attraction excludes sexual instinct and desire to have sexual relationship with opposite sex. Here, I mean the healthy desire to live or work with one another in a mutually happy and complimentary situation, sexual relationship is secondary. However, it is necessary to note that sexual relationship between man and woman is not a bad thing, otherwise God would not have placed the instinct in every human and indeed in everything that has flesh and blood. But just as in everything, what matters is the position it is placed in a relationship. It is the thought, the deeds and volition of a person that attracts other human beings of similar characteristics to the person. You will notice that top business executives think alike, just as professors and academics have their different line of thought form. You will notice that, if by any reason, people from diverse background are gathered in one large arena, you will soon observe this Law at work; groups of people form themselves, based on what they have in common- be it race, language, profession, religious or spiritual beliefs, political ideologies etc.

Applying this to marriage, it necessary that the most essential ingredient for a successful marriage is love between the two persons involved. This love does not fall from heaven and will, under no circumstance, fall from heaven. It is the complementary qualities of the couple that cements the love. This means that the couple can complement one another and be able to cope with each other's excesses. For instance, a woman that smokes will not give a damn if her husband is a chain smoker. In the same way, couple that share noble qualities will find it easy to live in perfect harmony; this will be so for they understand themselves and need each other's noble and complementary qualities to attain their maximum potential.

It is the natural Law of attraction of Homogeneous Species that will provide the magnetic force, which seems to attract and bind the two individuals together. Sometimes, it happens in such manner that the two persons could not remember how they began. All they could remember is that they just couldn't help but be stuck together. They can't afford to leave each other's side because they have some spiritual qualities that bind them together. Such relationship, whether in marriage or not, can be said to be made in Heaven. They can weather the storm when it hits them. So, it is necessary to say that there is no one person destined to marry a particular person. The criteria are the presence of those thoughts and deeds they have in common. These qualities must not be 80, 90 or 100% for the marriage to succeed but it has to be substantial enough. The higher the percentage of these common qualities, the more successful the marriage will be. Some persons may have thought that it was time to quit a relationship or marriage but on second thought and reassessment they will reconsider their action on the basis that there are other good qualities that can still sustain the marriage.

Some high profile marriages, such as those of Bill and Hilary Clinton and David and Victoria Beckam survived the turbulence that hit them because the parties involve needed each other. They are aware that there is nothing like perfect marriage or perfect person and were grateful for the gift of love they have been permitted to share from. And that, as long as they have a lot in common, both spiritually and materially, there is light at the end of the tunnel. The marriage between Barrack and Michelle Obama will meet quantum successes because they also have a great deal in common. From their common faith in God, to love and dedication to one's country, to their passion as voracious readers and compassionate writers, this marriage no doubt will have its challenges but it may not know serious pain.

From the above, it is to be expected that superficial persons who have neither spiritual values nor an understanding in the inner and finer qualities would be attracted to outward appearances, such as affluent background, skin color, physical looks, fashion, etc. Because such marriage is outward material things, it is most likely to be problematic once those physical and outward attractions begin to wane.

Marriage is made in Heaven is a saying that is as old as man. But marriages, as they are today and as they have always been for centuries, have so cast a shadow of doubt about this saying that many hardly believe it. Civil marriage is nothing more than a social or business contract. With few exceptions, many do not enter into marriage as willed by Creation. Genuine marriage is consummated with the intention of raising the inner and outer value of the persons concerned and in the process enabling them to strive together vigorously for high aims, thereby becoming a blessing to themselves, mankind and for further healthy development of Creation, generally. But marriage, as we consummate it today, is a simple bargain that ensures the material security of the parties involved.

The position of women in this arrangement is pitiable and degradable. In majority of cases, she enslaves herself to serve her husband who does not even seek in her a companion of equal worth, a tool and cheap housekeeper to make his home comfortable and to indulge his sensual appetite without hindrance.

Most young girls marry for most trivial reasons. Sometimes, it is simply to annoy or spite another girl who is already in love with the man or simply, in pursuit of material wealth, or because she is tired of staying at home. As a result, they rush so easily to uncalculated risk and unhappiness. Encouraged and aided by many parents, many young people do not let their intuition guide them on such important issues as marriage. This kind of false marriage has brought about serious retrogression.

What great difference when marriage is contracted on a healthy foundation and allowed to develop harmoniously, joyfully, jointly and voluntarily serving each of the partners and the couple grows upwards towards spiritual ennoblement. The result will be that, shoulder to shoulder, the partners, with smiling faces, will survive all mundane trials and move ahead courageously and come off victorious. It is therefore important that parents do not selfishly cajole their children into false marriages. Parents who do this are not only servants of self; they are transgressors of the Creator's immutable Laws, which will never go unpunished.

It is necessary to mention that marriage is truly made in Heaven only when the two persons involved complement each other in many respects. Here the spiritual qualities come first. At birth, every human brings about certain qualities. The upward ennoblement of these qualities lies in harmonious union with a person of opposite sex who has similar qualities. These qualities may not be identical but nevertheless complementary. And in complementing each other, they become full (one). That is, they attain their full value.

The above is fundamental to basic understanding of marriage. But this does not mean that, to each person, that there is only one particular or special person with whom one must enter into harmonious union but that there are generally several who possess the qualities to complement the other person. So Mr. Right or Miss Right is everywhere, no need for a person to wander for decades in search of a person's "missing rib".

Working together and having the same high aim in marriage is as important in marriage as water is for fish. For marriage to flourish there must be joint striving. There is no Lone Ranger in marriage; it is only in working together that the union will receive much higher consecration, which will bring real and strong spiritual blessing and protection.

Some may argue that the major ingredient for a successful marriage is Love between the two persons involved. This is equally true, but love does not fall from the sky. It is those complementary qualities that bind the couple together and develop Love which cement the union and make the couple inseparable, for in the real sense one can do without the other.

It should be noted that wherever one finds marriage that is linked in harmonious chord no one should do anything that will break the harmony or put the link asunder. The Natural Law of Creation forbids such putting asunder what the Will of the Almighty has joined together.

Some people do not necessarily appreciate good things until they see it in another person's hand. So, if you see a person that complements your quality and that the person is no longer available, do not attempt to put asunder any relationship that the person has developed elsewhere but keep your eyes and heart open. To your surprise, you will discover that there are several others that will equally make life beautiful and blissful for you.

Culture or tradition that does not incorporate the natural Laws of Creation simply becomes irrelevant. This is because such tradition was meant to serve selfish reasons. Take for instance the culture of Igbo people which today is one of the majority ethnic tribes in Nigeria. Culture and tradition vary from one community to the other in Igbo land but one aspect of that culture which has remained consistent and same all over is the culture of bride price in marriage. The culture decrees that once bride price is paid and accepted, the couple is considered married. In case of divorce, the bride's family has the options to return the bride price immediately or do so shortly after the bride marries a new husband. In cases whereby the bride price is not returned any child delivered by the woman whether in a new marriage or not belongs to the first (original) husband. Ordinarily, any culture taking a child away from the biological father is bad and unacceptable. Cultures like this are bad because it is self serving and in all cases those (women) that are adversely affected by these traditions are not part of the process of making the laws.

However, this tradition was not ordained for nothing. It was meant to encourage women to stay with one man. This culture has eaten deep into the lives of these people to the extent that divorce in marriage is to some extent considered taboo. Most fathers are ready to sacrifice anything to avoid having their married daughters return back to them. Moreover, families where their daughters are reputed for divorcing their husbands are seen as irresponsible and not good enough for suitors to enter. This cultural belief is further fortified by Christian belief that marriage, once contracted in accordance with Christian principles, is made in heaven and any separation under any circumstance amounts to putting asunder what God has joined together. Decrees like this are wrong and have led to unhappiness, untold hardship and enslavement of majority of women in the world today.

It is therefore important to argue that in cases where marriage is not working, and the union is not heading anywhere but disaster, it is better to encourage the persons involved to go their separate ways. This means that the marriage was superficially contracted in the first place. It will amount to the individuals concerned burdening themselves with guilt if they can no longer respect each other. Continued cohabitation of the persons who have lost love and respect for one another is immoral and the sexual relationship between them becomes nothing but adultery, very unhealthy even if such couple were joined in matrimony by the best churches.

Chapter 12

Tale of Two Marriages Gone Wrong

by: Azubike Aliche

He Blames it on Women's Greed,
She on Family Interference.

In the course of researching this book, we asked Igbo people who have had their marriages fail to discuss what they understand to be factors that contributed to the failure. What we discovered is that while each case is different, the environment in which these marriages operate impacted the stability of marriages, negatively. In other words, marriages that can survive in Igbo land can crash in the Diaspora, even when the same set of factors is at play. The other thing that we found out, as reflected in the two stories published below, is that when it comes to what things that cause problems in marriages, men and women see it differently. The reader is advised that the names used in this story – Okoro and Ugochi – are fictitious and that these are only one side of the stories in which two or more people were actors.

Okoro's Case: Blame it on Greed!

When Okoro called me that Tuesday, late in the morning, as I prepared to go to work, I wanted to give him a new date and time to talk but his first few words and the heavy emotions that I sensed behind them made me change my mind and stayed glued to the phone until he finished almost an hour later. He was virtually crying, which is not common for Igbo men. And this is for a man who is approaching 60 years of age and has married twice (he lives with his second wife). I didn't get the exact information on how long Okoro has lived in the United States but he was already working in a correctional facility, as far back as 1991. The most painful thing for Okoro is that his daughter from the failed marriage is in college and he does not even know which college and where. They have not been in contact for years, one consequence of the demise of his first marriage. And his second marriage has not produced an offspring. According to him, it appears that this wife does not accord childbearing as much importance as he does, which worsens his worries. That he lost his preferred job and drives a cab now pales into nothing, compared with his pain that he can't be with any of his children or have more, at least for now.

Okoro said he called after reading my solicitation message. He explained that he wanted to write to give me the information that I need but felt that writing will worsen his depression. He said he felt better talking on the phone about his misfortune with marriage. Apart from losing contact with his children from the first marriage, he has child support arrears to deal with, he said. He's just secured a lawyer to help him seek modification of his child support order. He is virtually unemployed as we spoke and stays home much of the day, apparently a symptom of depression. He's trained in a mental health field and had years of work experience in the field but he is not licensed or certified as a mental health professional. He's considering alternative employment in Nigeria, through a nonprofit organization that he founded but he needs to raise grant money first.

According to Okoro, there was no domestic violence involved in the marriage, which explains why he's upset that his wife left. Okoro is particularly upset that his ex-wife fabricated stories against him to find an excuse to end the marriage and leave with their daughters. He thinks this is a wicked act. "If you hate me, why not ask that we share what we have and part in peace, instead of fabricating something that did not happen, he asked rhetorically. He said that the woman had told authorities that he threw her out of the window from a second floor of a building. Okoro stated that his mother-in-law was implicated in the conspiracy to end his marriage.

Okoro was unequivocal that greed was behind the action of the woman he married for about six years. Someone had introduced the woman to him to set the stage for the marriage. He recalled that he had to put his own education on hold to support his ex-wife to get a master's degree before he got his. "Greed ... Greed... Greed, he chanted! He noted that he personally went to Nigeria to bring his mother-in-law, the same woman he accuses of conspiring with her daughter to dissolve his marriage. When Okoro continued to stress that his current wife works long hours so she can send money to her parents, rather than spend time at home to see if the couple will conceive a child, he implies that greed is still at work.

Ugochi: The Culprit is Family Interference!

Ugochi's story is really very interesting, to the extent that it provides a contrast to Okoro's. Here is a case in which the woman insists that she got nothing from her husband before the breakup and subsequent divorce, except of course the children she had from him. Ugochi reported that she paid her way to meet her husband here, using nonimmigrant visa. Many times, when people, particularly men, discuss what women gain when their husbands file for immigrant visas and bring them over here, they leave out the sacrifices or hardship that some of these women go through before arriving here or even after. In the case of Ugochi, here was a young woman who set her eyes on higher education and had secured admission to university in London when she was pressured to marry. She and her husband had already married when her ex-husband left for the United States. For 10 years or so, she remained in Nigeria without furthering her education and when she came here, her ex-husband decided she had to be home full time, as housewife. And he took no steps to help her regularize her stay in the United States. Instead, Ugochi says, her ex-husband sabotaged her efforts in this direction by hiding the documents that she needed to pursue her application for permanent residence.

Although Ugochi speaks of disappointment with her ex, she does not hold him squarely responsible for their broken marriage. She blames her sister-in-law for interfering in what should be the business of the couple. She noted that the said sister-in-law would come to her home and fight her. She believes that when her ex-husband packed his things in a truck and left the house and never returning, it was at the instruction of his older sister. And what annoyed Ugochi the most is that her ex-husband refused to take their son with him or allow him to visit. This had led to anger and behavior issues for the youth, at the time. To be fair to her parents-in-law, Ada gives them credit for standing by her throughout her ordeal but their efforts was not sufficient to move her ex on their side.

Ugochi, whose father learned to read and write in his adult years, painted a picture of herself as an ambitious youngster, prior to her adventure into marriage. Her goal was to attain self-actualization in life through formal education. She had planned to do this by studying law or journalism. She dreamed of becoming a broadcaster in Nigeria. She had family and friends in London and the United States who inspired and encouraged her to pursue her passion – higher education. Early marriage put all of that on hold. Early marriage robbed her of a chance to study in London where a relative of hers had secured her admission into a school. She had become pregnant before her husband left for the US. She lived with her husband's family in Nigeria for a number of years, before moving out when her relationship with her sister-in-law had gone sour. She lived the life of single mother in Nigeria where she was a high school teacher while raising her son. Little did she know that she will return to the status of a single mother, again, after a stint in marriage here in the United States. Two years after she arrived in the US, Ugochi got pregnant again.

Ugochi, who presents as someone who subscribes to traditional gender ideology, said that she gave her husband all the money she made from her first job but apparently this did not change much in their frosty relationship. Ironically, the support that Ugochi could not find in her husband, she found with a kind-hearted American woman, Shirley, who doubled as her employer. Shirley helped Ugochi with getting a lawyer who filed papers for her permanent residence. She also supported Ugochi so she could train as a nurse. Another woman was to offer to care for Ugochi's newborn for the entire period that she was in school. Interestingly, Ugochi's ex-husband had pressured her to abort this baby when the couple first found out that they were expecting the child. When her husband packed his property and left, only a television set, a box spring bed and couch were left in the apartment and Ugochi had two months to pack out or face ejection from the landlord. She did leave, having secured an efficiency apartment just on time before the expiration date of their subsisting lease.

Ugochi emphasizes that when it comes to the reasons why marriages develop problems, each case is different. She says that, in some cases, the problem begins when people marry for money. She cites examples of people who go back to Igbo land to marry nurses in the expectation that they would make money for them here, instead of marrying someone they love who may not be a nurse. Frustration or even anger sets in when the money does not come in the amount that they expected. She also says that, on the other hand, some women marry as a passport to come to America, so they can make money for themselves and their families. Trouble comes when they find that who they married is the "controlling type." Whatever the case is, she says, when a woman works up to 60 hours or more per week, as some do, "her role as a wife is endangered." She added that it is challenging for a woman to combine household duties with long work hours and the stress associated with it.

Chapter 13

The 12 "Disciples"

by: Azubike Aliche and Stella Nwokeji

Who they are, what they earn, how they Resolve Marital Conflict and why their Marriages Succeeded or Failed!

It's often said of Christ's disciples that many were called but few were chosen. In our own case, only 12 people chose to respond to our survey instrument, posted on the Internet for over six months, for the public. However, what we lacked in numbers, we got in the high quality of the responses. In terms of demographics and variety of opinions and experiences shared, the diversity is enriching. One outstanding fact of the result of our survey is the place of the family in the stability or otherwise of Igbo marriages in the United States. Second to that is the role that money and its handling plays in making and unmaking our marriages. There are many other interesting findings, including the fact that the ethnic origin of the partners in a marriage can have an impact on the health of that marriage. Because of its small sample size, we shall leave to the reader the question of whether the findings can be generalized for all Igbo marriages in the United States. One thing is clear, though: To a large extent, the Igbo is a largely homogenous group in the United States.

Who are our 12 disciples?

Our respondents comprise of seven women and five men. Four of our respondents are of Abia State origin; six are of Imo State origin. One respondent originally came from Anambra, while the other came from Anioma (Delta State). In terms of how long they have lived in the United States, which can affect acculturation, they have lived anywhere from 14 to 37 years, with more than half having lived here 20 years or more. When it comes to the reason that they came to the United States, originally, half said that they had come to join their families; three said they came in search of better life, while two had come to pursue the Golden Fleece (education). One person came because she benefitted from the Diversity Visa Lottery. A further breakdown shows that all the women, except the visa lottery beneficiary, reported that they had come to join their spouses. Usually, their spouses would have filed a petition for immigrant visas for them and they arrive as US permanent residents, after a process that can take up to two years and lots of money and anxiety.

Half of our respondents are in the 42-51-year-old age bracket. Four or one-third are in the 52-61- year-old age bracket and two in the 32-41-year-old age bracket. A further analysis shows that all the women, but one, who responded were 51 years old or younger. They were also younger than their husbands, which is usually the case with the Igbo, even in the motherland. Four of our respondents attended some college; two had bachelor's degree; two have master's degrees; one has a post-master's certification while three hold doctorate degrees. All of those who indicated that they have some college experience are females. One female respondent has a master's degree while one has a doctorate degree. Of all 12 respondents, nine reported that they hold professional licenses in their field of specialty. Of the two who don't, one is a woman while the other is a man. One woman and two men among our respondents listed "service or skilled worker," as their occupational status, while the rest report that they belong to the Administration/Management/professional cadre.

Eight of our respondents are married. Among these are all five men and three women. The other four who are single, divorced or separated are women. One of the men reported that he was divorced 15 years ago. Two of our men respondents are in their second marriage. One of our divorcee respondents married for 18 years before the divorce. Interestingly, every one of our respondents is marrying an Igbo or has married an Igbo in the past. Our questionnaire included a question asking respondents how long they have been married but only four people responded, with all of them having married a minimum of 10 years each. The longest married person in the group, a man, has married for 28 years. Another married man has married for 27 years.

Of our female respondents, two are of the same age bracket with their husbands, while three are of a lower age group than their husbands'. Three of the five male respondents are older than their wives; one is about the same age as his wife while one man did not disclose the age of his partner.

Factors Affecting the Quality of Marriage

On the question of what factor(s) has affected the quality of their marital relationships, an overwhelming majority (10 out of 12) indicated that "shared ethnicity" was the most crucial. A man and a woman did not choose this factor from the list provided. Five of 12 stated that "identical goals and values" with their partners was important. Five of 12 chose "open and honest relationship." Underscoring the role of the family in Igbo marriage, at home and abroad, seven out of twelve stated that when "marriage enjoys the support of both spouse's families" the chance of success was greater. Only two of 12 (one man and one woman) chose the option of "compatible temperament and personality" as crucial to the success in their marriages. Could this be a reason why western-style courtship is not usually part of Igbo marriage processes?

Ways of Resolving Conflict in Marriage

We asked for their preferred method of resolving family or interpersonal conflict. To this, all but one female, responded that they do that "by ourselves in the confines of our home." This appears to be the safest and result-oriented method. In addition to this method of conflict resolution, three others chose "religion-oriented counseling by priests/religious leaders." The Igbo in the motherland and in the Diaspora are predominantly Christians. Three others chose "counseling and mediation by our parents, again, underscoring the place of the family in the stability of marriages. Four chose "by eliciting mediation from our close friends."

Interestingly, everyone shunned the more formal, social services-oriented "conventional American human services and social services counseling," as a means to resolving marital conflicts. In the same way, no one touched the other choices available in the questionnaire:

"With the help of friendly neighbors," probably because these neighbors are likely to be Americans. Many Igbo people like their American neighbors and can socialize with them but when it comes to trusting them with their private matters, few Igbo are willing to do that. Many Americans can't keep things secret the way Igbo do and may easily report to the authorities for resolution what many Igbo would rather settle in a different manner.

"Intervention and counseling of community elders," perhaps out of concern that confidentiality cannot be guaranteed by these elders compared with, for example, priests/religious leaders. Although many elders in Igbo land are good at keeping things private and confidential, it is arguable whether the elders here embrace that value, particularly after many years in America, with all the phone facilities and other means of communication with which people interact. Many Igbo always live with the fear of what is called *asiri* (gossip), an informal, underground system of communication in which people discuss something they would not talk about openly but which can eventually come to light or damage the subject of that gossip without their knowing. Most people who engage in *asiri* would tend to disclose or discuss the subject matter in confidence with a trusted person but the danger is that that trusted person has other trusted persons with who they may share the information and the process goes on, until most people get to know about it. Although elders are supposed to have outgrown *asiri*, many are not comfortable to entrust their private matter to others they don't know enough, even if they are by age considered elders in the community. That appears to be the reason that people would confide marital problems in their close friends rather than community elders they may not know well enough.

Money Matters: Household Incomes and More

We asked our respondents about their household incomes, just in case this factors in how their marriages are performing. What we found is that all our female respondents, except one, reported a family annual income of less than $100,000.00. Three of the male respondents reported household incomes above $100,000.00. Two reported incomes under $50,000.00 per year. All our respondents, except one, reported that theirs were two-income families in which the spouses work. One male respondent who made less than $50,000.00 reported that his wife was unemployed. This is understandable, since he reported that while they have married for 28 years; his wife joined him in the USA only in 2011. He's been in the United States since 1994. That's how long some families can be separated for the sake of making a better life in the USA. It is interesting that even though he's the only income earner, this respondent reported that when it comes to handling money in the home "we make decisions involving money jointly," "we operate a joint bank account," and "handling money is not an issue in my family."

Three of seven female respondents earned more than their husbands. Two of five male respondents earned more than their wives. Two of the five men earned less than their spouses. One man did not report who earns more. Ironically, the man who earned less than his spouse earned a master's degree, while his wife earned a bachelor's. He was divorced 15 years ago. For money handling, he reported that the two "operate separate bank accounts, with each spouse contributing equally or proportionately towards family projects," then "each spouse does his/her financial thing." On how disagreements are resolved, he chose the options "by ourselves in the confines of our home," and "by eliciting mediation from close friends." On why his first marriage failed, he listed "lack of trust," "spouse does not want children," "spouse not loyal to my family of origin," and "intrusion/meddling by extended family members." He initiated the divorce in the first marriage. Incidentally, he still does not have children with his current wife.

In the case of one of the women who reported that they earn more than their husbands, she reports, for money handling, that "we operate separate bank accounts," and that "each spouse does his or her financial thing." However, she added that "my spouse makes financial decisions. One way to understand this is to see that she had indicated that "each spouse contributes equally or proportionately towards family projects." So, it appears that, once she gives her husband her own share of a project or budget, she does not bother about how the money is spent. This may be to avoid arguments or to cede authority to her husband, as is traditional with Igbo people. In fact, the two other women who earn more than their husbands each reported that they keep separate accounts from their husbands. The data size is too small to make a conclusion whether this is a trend that women who earn more than their husbands tend to keep a separate bank account. This is more so when the other four women who reported that they earned less than their husbands were split in the middle, with two reporting separate account and the other two reporting joint bank account with their husbands.

On the whole, seven of our 12 respondents operate separate bank accounts from their spouses, while five operate joint account. Five of those who reported separate bank account are women. One man reported that while he and his spouse operate separate bank accounts, they also have a joint bank account in which the partners pay in their part of the family expenses. For that account, decision about how to manage it is made jointly.

Why their Marriages Failed

Four of our respondents are either divorced, separated or have experienced divorce from their partners in the past. Below are the reasons that they chose from the list provided, as contributing factors to the death of their marriages. They had a chance to include more reasons from outside those provided but they did not use that chance.

Divorcee #1:

Dishonesty, incompatible personality and/or temperament, money, spouse not loyal to my family of origin, and intrusion or meddling by extended family members.

Divorcee #2:

Incompatible personality and/or temperament, money, spouse not loyal to family of origin, and intrusion or meddling by extended family.

Divorcee #3

Mutual dissatisfaction, divergent and conflicting goals, incompatible values, money, spouse not loyal to family of origin, intrusion or meddling by extended family members.

Divorcee #4

Lack of trust, spouse does not want children, spouse not loyal to my family of origin, intrusion or meddling by extended family members.

The Place of the Family in Marriage

Often, it is assumed that disagreements over how to handle money earned in the family is the primary source of discord in Igbo marriages in the Diaspora, particularly given that nurses who often earn more than their husbands are targets for domestic violence, going by the media reports reviewed in the literature. In our survey though, what we see is that money actually comes behind the family and the sentiments that the Igbo attach to their family of origin, in relation to their family of procreation. You can think of it in terms of the extended family versus the immediate (nuclear) family. Unlike Westerners, it does appear that even in their nuclear families in industrialized Western countries, the extended family continues to exert a pull or push for Igbo couples to the extent that their marriages could be in jeopardy.

When it comes to the factors that contributed to the breakup of their marriages, our respondents, all four divorcees included "spouse not loyal to my family of origin" and "intrusion or meddling by extended family members." Of all the 12 possible factors listed in the questionnaire, only money comes close, by garnering three points. If this is considered alongside our question on what contributes to the quality of marital relationship and in which a majority listed "marriage enjoys the support of both spouses' families, it can further be seen how the extended family can be a factor in cohesion, just as it can be in division. This seems to confirm that the Igbo tradition of seeing marriage as a union of two families, instead of two adults, is still alive and well. The message here is that spouses are expected to "marry" everyone in the other partner's family or neglect that at the peril of the whole relationship.

Profiles

We offer a closer look at three of our respondents, so that readers can see if there is something to learn from them, in terms of how they are managing their married lives or why their marriages have succeeded or failed. It is not your typical case study, as we do not plan to draw any conclusions from their stories.

Rather, all we want to do is offer information and leave our readers to draw any inferences that they may. The three represent a woman who reported that she and her spouse each have doctoral degrees and earn about the highest annual household income among our respondents, another woman who is divorced and a man who has married the longest (28 years) among our respondents.

The doctors in the house

Our Ph.D. holder who is Christian came to United States in 1995 to join her husband who is a medical doctor. She has been here 16 years but she reports that adjustment was not easy in her early years. As for her experience settling down in the USA, she reports that it was "not easy but somewhat I was able to adapt to the American culture." She believes that her social status hasn't been much different from what it was in Nigeria. In terms of age, she's somewhere between 32 and 41 years old. In terms of occupational status, she places herself in the administration/management/professional cadre. This is her first marriage, married to an Igbo man for 16 years now. Her husband is older, in the 52-61 years age bracket.

She reported that marrying an Igbo man with who she shares compatible temperament and personality has helped their marriage, just as the fact that their marriage enjoys the support of families on both sides of the marriage. If the couple has a problem in their marriage, she and her husband resolve it by themselves in the confines of their home. With her husband, they make a minimum of $500,000 per year. Her husband makes more of this money than she does. She says of how they handle money in the house: "We make decisions involving money jointly. We operate a joint bank account. Handling money is not an issue in my family." The couple has four children, ranging in age from 10 to 15 years. There is no behavior or academic problems to report for their children.

The Tried and Tested

They have married for 28 years but lived separately for 17 year, as husband adjusts to the demand of living in the United States. She joined him only in 2011. He left her in Nigeria in 1994. Despite the interruption, though, the marriage remains strong. He reported that he had come here in search of better life, for himself and family. He ranks his social status higher in the US, compared with what it was in Nigeria. He holds a bachelors degree, acquired in Nigeria. He reports this as his second marriage, apparently because he had to marry here due to the exigencies of living in America. Some Igbo have had to marry someone, divorce them and remarry the same person, as circumstances demand. This appears to be one of those cases. He reported that his wife graduated high school and currently is looking for employment. One thing that has been helping their marriage, in the last 28 years, is that the marriage enjoys the support of both of their families. When problems arise, they settle it by themselves in the confines of their house. Although he is the only one working, and earns under $50,000 per annum, he still has a joint bank account with his wife and makes spending decisions jointly with her. He states that "handling money is not an issue in my family." The couple has four children together who are doing well in behavior and educational achievement.

Single Again!

She married for 18 years! Then she became single! When she arrived the shores of the United States in 1990, she had come to join her husband. What she saw on arrival "exceeded her expectations." She finds that she enjoys a higher social status here in the US, compared with what obtained in Nigeria. She reported that "overall, I find that there are enough community-based resources to meet my unique needs. She should know because she has a special needs child. She may also have used social/legal service help in the course of her divorce but information on this was not asked for in the questionnaire.

She's somewhere in age between 42 and 51 years old. She holds a master's degree and states that she works as a service or skilled worker. Her ex-husband is older, as he fell in the 52-61-year age bracket. But, with a bachelor's degree, he attained a lower educational height than our respondent. It's not clear from her reports if this played a part in their divorce, particularly because he earned more money. Apparently because she's the only one in the household earning money, she reported her household income to be in the range of $51,000 – 100,000. She earned about the same amount of money as her ex-husband. There was no question in the questionnaire that asked if she gets child support payments, spousal support or some kind of public/social security payments for her disabled child. She did not answer the question about whether this is her first, second or third marriage but information she volunteered suggests that she or her ex-husband may have married more than once, as she reported that of the five children they have three comes from her husband's first marriage.

Although she's now single, she still answered questions about quality of marital relationship and conflict resolution in marriage, apparently relying on her experience while she was married. She states that "shared ethnicity" and "identical values and goals" among partners was crucial to improving the quality of marital relationship. In terms of how she resolved conflicts with her ex-husband, she states that involved "eliciting mediation from close friends," using "religion-oriented counseling by priests and religious leaders," as well as using the counseling and mediation that their parents provided. In discussing what factors contributed to the failure of her marriage, she cited "mutual dissatisfaction," "divergent and conflicting goals," "incompatible values," "money," "spouse not loyal to my family of origin" and "intrusion by extended family members." It is interesting to note that her ex-husband initiated the divorce.

Chapter 14

This Works for Me

by: Stella Nwokeji and Azubike Aliche

The culture war that the Igbo in the Diaspora fight, no doubt, leaves many marriages scarred. However, a great majority of Igbo marriages survive, with little or no impact. In realization of this fact, the authors of this book decided to bring together a focus group to discuss what works for Igbo couples who have succeeded in their marriages. On December 30, 2011, 17 people called in to a teleconference during which they shared their experiences and perspectives on what works for them and could work for others. Five men and five women actively participated. Among these was Uju Nwobodo, a young Igbo woman who has been married for seven years. She was born in Nigeria but raised in the United States. Her husband who called in briefly was born and raised in Nigeria. There was, also, Okechukwu Onyeizu, a young Igbo man who was born and raised in Nigeria until he came over to pursue university education. He's been married for three years. On the other side of the age spectrum was Lolo Evelyn Nwigwe who has been married for up to 30 years and has adult children. There was also a man who holds traditional chieftaincy title. He would not want his name be used for this article. All participants have college or advanced degrees and are Christians. Their states of origin in Nigerian include, Abia, Anambra, Ebonyi, Enugu, Imo, and Delta. The other participants were born and raised in Nigeria, just as their spouses. All participants but one live in the United States and have a minimum of one child. One participant called in from Canada.

This diversity in the focus group ensured that the best of what works for various age groups was produced, at the end of the exercise. While the responses are not meant to be generalized, we hope that people will find them useful when they adapt them to their own situations.

All the responses were analyzed for common themes. The following responses occurred most frequently.

WHAT WORKS IN IGBO MARRIAGES?

- Compatibility among spouses, as it relates to personality, priorities, shared values.
- Know who you are marrying.
- Unconditional love, trust, and mutual respect.
- Cultivate love where none exist.
- Goal-oriented partnership in marriage.
- Communication among couples where there is a misunderstanding.
- Conflict resolution between the couples involved without third party interference.
- Ability of the male to take up the responsibility as the head of the household including financial, child rearing responsibilities to mention but a few.
- The reason for getting into the marriage was pure on love and not material or financial freedom.
- Ability to make out time to attend church as a family and also pray as a

family.

- Keeping in mind what marriage means in Igbo culture.
- Ability of the women to understand and work with their spouses when there are projects to be done at home in Nigeria.
- When couples speak with one voice and execute projects as "we did" instead of "I did this."
- Making out time for each other, irrespective of your busy schedules.
- Understanding gender role change when a woman becomes the bread winner.
- Respect for the in-laws.
- Do not be stagnant, change with the environment (Marriage in Igbo land is a man's world while it is a woman's world in America or most of the western world).
- Mediation Committees set up in different cities where anonymous volunteers intervene to resolve marriage conflicts to avoid divorce.

WHAT FACTORS CAUSE CONFLICTS IN IGBO MARRIAGES?

- Marriage of convenience (to get out of Nigeria or to get into marriage to help family)
- Lack of love or respect for each other.
- "Nuclear marriage" where extended family, including in-laws, are excluded.
- Mixed message among spouses when it relates to their in-laws.
- Parents-in-law's disrespect for their son or daughter in-laws.
- Generational age gap in couples.
- Lack of prayers in homes.
- Males falling short of their household responsibilities.
- Lack of division of labor. When a woman becomes the bread winner and at the same time is expected to do all household chores.
- Lack of gender role changes to reflect the condition of the family. A situation where a man stays at home doing nothing but expects wife to still satisfy him sexually after long hours at work.
- Treats partner as an "ATM machine," particularly a nurse wife, and decides not to contribute financially in the home.
- Keeps long hours in community meetings without making time to spend with family.
- Conflict among couples over money issues.
- Notion that all women must give sex freely to their spouses, no matter the circumstance.

- When women use sex as object of revenge.
- When a man or woman is not able to satisfy the other spouse, sexually.
- Exposure of family problems to friend, parents, and siblings. Here, when the couple reconciles, the family member may still bear grudges for the man or woman for maltreating their son or daughter.

Here is a sampling of the statements that the respondents offered:

"There should be love between the partners. People should not marry strangers, for any reason. There should be respect for the family (on both sides); respect for our culture and respect for the man, as head of the family. Our women should learn to assume the wife's role and our men should accept that women can make more money than they can. Respect for one another is important, as our kids are watching. We don't have to change or adapt to every culture, as the chameleon changes its color. Couples should have priorities and keep them."

"People should be careful as they select marriage partners. We need to understand who we are and what we are getting into. I've been married for three years. I had my priorities about the kind of person I wanted to marry. I wanted to be sure that I get someone whose lifestyle is compatible with mine. Christian values and Biblical perspectives should bear on marriage. You have to want God to be part of your marriage. Some people have dropped all the things they came in (from Nigeria) with. Bring God into your midst"

"Compromise is needed. Don't try to change your partner. Find out your partner's strengths and focus on that; do not focus on weaknesses. You can't change anybody. Even courtship doesn't guarantee success in marriage. Couples grew up in different environments and this affects who they are and what they bring to the relationship. In the past, dad was the breadwinner while mom was housewife. Now, most wives are working and cannot be expected to do everything (chores) in the house, as our mothers did. A woman cannot play the role of breadwinner, wife and housewife, simultaneously. America is a woman's world while Africa is a man's world. Don't be rigid; to men, I say be flexible. Also, sexual compatibility is important. It can stabilize marriage."

"It takes both men and women to make it work! You don't take what you do in your father's house to go to your husband's house. Success of a marriage can depend on how the woman respects her husband and how the man handles it. Couples should respect one another. Good communication skill is important. We must know that we are Igbos and that our culture emphasizes respect for the husband and elders. We should know the right ways to resolve conflict."

"Go into marriage for the right reasons. People should understand each other before marriage. Don't choose a partner on the basis of income, position, etc. Ensure that your ego and that of your partner is intact.

"Sexual relationship and satisfaction is a two-way thing. Couples should work to meet each other's sexual needs."

"Men should help in the house with such things as child care, cooking, etc., and not sit in front of the computer or TV all day. It doesn't change the man's status, as the head of the family. It's the role of the man to take care of his wife, in whatever way necessary."

"The impression that couples give to their parents about their partners affect the attitude of family members to their partners. Couples should speak in one voice when it comes to what to do with in-laws. The only way that someone can interfere in your marriage is if you give them a chance. Make decisions together. Don't tell in-laws anything about your marriage and relationship. Couples should be open to one another; don't hide anything."

"The man should go out there and make money and not wait for the woman to make the money. Don't hide money. Each marriage is unique. What works for one couple may not work for another. See yourself as unique and be satisfied with what you have, as a couple. Women should respect their husband's people, her in-laws. It's hard for the marriage, if a wife has issues with her in-laws."

What works

By Chime Okafor

These are my feelings as to what could work with Igbo couples here in USA.

1. We must learn to be honest with each other, regarding our finances; because it should not matter who makes the most money, if all is well in the marriage. Sit down and plan better ways to manage your funds better. Don't hide any separate account; be honest about it because it is good to have one joint account and then individual accounts in every marriage.

2. There must be room for open communication and respect for each other. No yelling and no putting down each other, especially when the children are around. Children do not want to hear that their father is not doing well or that their mother is not a good mother because it hurts their spirit.

3. We, as women, must understand that, no matter how unproductive our husbands are, they are still the head of the household, according to the word of God, and our culture. Some of us understand that some men are not what they seem when you meet them before marriage, but so are some of us women. It does not take away a man's position in the household just because you are making more money than him.

4. Husbands should have better control over their households and be the "man" and play the role because when you surrender that position to your wife then you will never get it back. Also, please keep your mothers and sisters out of your marriages. Women, we must remember that we have parents, too. Therefore, we must treat our in-laws as we would like our parents to be treated. No double standard.

5. Please, we must never use our children or sex against our partners. Sex is

everywhere and you may not like the outcome when you send your mate outside for sex. Know also that when you use the children against each other, they will end up hating you. Sometimes, when there is a problem in marriages, wives and husbands start to inject bias in the minds of the innocent children which confuses them. Children do not want to hear that their mother is a prostitute, (that is the only thing men use against women that hurts us) while the women will tell the children that their father is not a good provider; he is lazy, and he has all kinds of women outside the home, etc. Men must not beat their wives in the presence of their children nor should women call their husbands names in the presence of their children. It hurts even the children when they hear that.

6. Being a good listener plays a major role in the success of every relationship. Men must not treat their wives as house girls who cannot contribute ideas to the running of the home. Couples should not talk over each other. I know that we, as women, are good at doing that, because we know that it annoys the men. It is wrong. Women, when you ask for the truth, be prepared for the truth. However, if you can't stand the truth, do not ask for it.

7. Finally, bear in mind that it is not all about you, is about "WE" and not "I" any more.

• Chime Okafor, LMSW, is a social worker in New York.

Chapter 15

State of Domestic Violence in the United States

by: Azubike Aliche

In order to put the contents of this book in proper perspective, it is imperative to look at relevant statistics and information regarding the prevalence of domestic violence in the United States, our host country and culture. To this end, we have reviewed and adapted information from the surveys conducted by the Bureau of Justice Statistic (BJS).The official name for this is the BJS National Crime Victimization Survey (NCVS) The survey covered data collected from residents living throughout the United States, including persons living in group quarters, such as dormitories, rooming houses, and religious group dwellings. We have also used other information from databases maintained for the Federal Bureau of Investigations (FBI). In some cases, we have reproduced these data verbatim, as contained in the report. In other cases, we have rephrased them to bring the meanings out, more clearly. Please, note that there is frequent reference to family violence, which is not necessarily the same as domestic violence or intimate partner violence. The report refers to family violence as including "all types of violent crime by an offender who is related to the victim either biologically or legally through marriage or adoption." It also went on to state that "a crime is considered family violence if the victim was the offender's current or former spouse; parent or adoptive parent; current or former stepparent; legal guardian; biological or adoptive child; current or former stepchild; sibling; grandchild; current or former step- or adoptive-grandchild; grandparent; current or former step- or adoptive-grandparent; in-law; or other relative (aunt, uncle, nephew)." Because of the nature and focus of our book, we have paid more attention to information related to spousal abuse or violence. These statistics may not represent the latest data on the subject matter but they form a good basis for putting some of the issues in the book in their proper perspectives. Indications are that overall, intimate partner violence is falling. For example, the rate of intimate partner violence against females declined 53% between 1993 and 2008, from 9.4 victimizations per 1,000 females age 12 or older to 4.3 per 1,000. Against males, the rate declined 54%, from 1.8 victimizations per 1,000 males age 12 or older to 0.8 per 1,000. Here is what we have:

- Family violence accounted for 11 percent of all reported and unreported violence between 1998 and 2002. This comes down to about 3.5 million violent crimes that people committed against their family members.

- Forty-nine percent of the 3.5 million violent crimes committed against family members were committed against spouses. That means that one partner in a couple relationship committed the crime against the other partner.

- Simple assault turned out to be the most frequent type of family violence that occurred during the period in reference (1998-2002). The least frequent, standing at one percent, is murder.

- Of the 3.5 million victims of family violence, between 1998 and 2002, less than one percent died as a result of the incident.

- Females constituted 84 percent of spouse abuse victims, making them the majority.

- About three-quarters of the persons who committed family violence were male.

- Most family violence victims were white (74 percent). Most family violence offenders were white (79 percent). We did not find the statistics for African (Igbo) immigrants who constitute a small percentage of the US population.

- About 22 percent of murders in 2002 were family murders. Nearly nine percent were murders of a spouse.

- Females were 58 percent of family murder victims. Of all the murders of females in 2002, family members were responsible for 43 percent. Please, note that family murder is not the same as murder by a spouse. It could have been by a spouse, a son, daughter, or other family member.

- Eighty percent of murderers who killed a family member were male. Males are responsible for 83 percent of the cases in which someone murdered a spouse.

- Approximately, 60 percent of family violence victimization was reported to police between 1998 and 2002.

- In 34 percent of the cases, victims of family violence failed to report the incidents to the police because they think it was a "private/personal matter." Another 12 percent of the victims of family violence failed to report the violence because they thought it was important to "protect the offender."

- A little over two million incidents of family violence were reported to police between 1998 and 2002. In 36 percent of these incidents, police made arrests.

- In the year 2000, family violence constituted one-third (33 percent) of all violent crimes (207,000) recorded by police in 18 states and the District of Columbia. Of all the family violence incidents (207,000), about half (110,000 or 53 percent) were crimes between spouses.

- Among crimes reported to police, two percent of family violence involved a firearm, compared to six percent of nonfamily violence. A weapon (not necessarily firearm) was used in 16 percent of family violence, as against 21 percent of nonfamily violence.

143

- In the year 2000, about 49 percent of family violence crimes recorded by police resulted in an arrest. Males constituted 77 percent of suspected family violence offenders arrested in that year.

- State courts sentenced 83 percent of persons convicted of assault (both family and nonfamily) to either prison or jail. Of this population, 68 percent of those incarcerated for family assault went to jail.

- Forty-five percent of persons sent to prison for family assault received a sentence of more than two years.

- While the bulk of domestic violence cases are handled at state court levels, federal prosecution of domestic violence cases do occur.

- Between 2000 and 2002, 757 suspected cases of domestic violence were referred to U.S. attorneys for prosecution. Most of these cases involved the use of firearms. Others involved interstate domestic violence offenses, with the FBI investigating and referring to US attorneys.

- Federal courts convicted 90 percent of defendants appearing before them on charges of interstate domestic violence offenses.

- Of the 47 Federal defendants sentenced for an interstate domestic violence offense between 2000 and 2002, 91 percent received a prison term with a median length of five years. This suggests that the penalty for domestic violence may be stiffer at the federal level.

- For the year 1997, about 90 percent of offenders in State prisons for family violence had injured their victims. Fifty percent of family violence victims were raped or sexually assaulted. Twenty-eight percent of the victims of family violence were killed and fifty percent of offenders in State prisons for spousal abuse had killed their victims.

- With regard to gender, females were more likely than males to be victimized by family violence. They are also more likely to be victimized by specific types of family violence. Females were about 50 percent of all spouses and romantic partners in the US but they represent 84.6 percent of spouse abuse victims. About men, between 1998 and 2002, four out of five violent offenders were male. Males accounted for 75.6 percent of family violence offenders. Also, among violent crimes against a spouse, 86.1 percent of the offenders were male.

- By racial categories, whites and blacks were more likely than Hispanics or persons of other races to be victimized by family violence. Between 1998 and 2002, non-Hispanic whites were 72.9 percent of the U.S. population age 12 or older but 74 percent of family violence victims. Non-Hispanic blacks were 12.1 percent of the population age 12 and older but 13.6 percent of family violence victims. Corresponding figures for the persons of other races were 4.1 percent of the 12 or older population and 2.3 percent of family violence victims. Between 1998 and 2002, among family violence offenders, 78.5 percent were white, 14.9 percent were black, and 6.6 percent were some other race.

- It is important to note that domestic violence can still occur even when no physical injury has been inflicted on the victim. Verbal threat to hurt the victim is considered violence. Even attempts to physically harm the victim, as in the cases where the victim flees from the scene, constitute violence. Of the 32.2 million victims of violent crimes between 1998 and 2002, only about one-quarter of this number sustained an injury. An estimated 19.5 percent of family violence cases involved an offender with a weapon. A weapon can include a gun, a knife, some other sharp object (such as scissors or an ice pick), or a blunt object (such as a rock, stick or baseball bat).

- Although family violence comprised 11 percent of all the 32.2 million violent crimes from 1998 to 2002, family violence victims made up 15.2 percent of the injured victims. This suggests that the likelihood is higher that a family violence will result in an injury, compared to nonfamily violence. Victims of spouse violence constituted 5.4 percent of all victims but 7.8 percent of injured victims.

- The other contributing factor to family violence appears to be the influence of drug and alcohol. In the NCVS survey under reference for the period 1998 to 2002, 38.5 percent of family violence victims reported that the offender was under the influence of drugs or alcohol during the incidents.

Epilogue

Why They Kill Their Wives!

by: Azubike Aliche

Media reports that some Igbo men killed their wives, who happened to be nurses, triggered work on this book. When I thought of writing directly on this phenomenon in which a man would kill his wife and mother of his children, my initial reaction was to restrain myself. As a mental health clinician, my instinct is to say that I couldn't make any informed comment, unless I had completed a full assessment of these individuals who allegedly killed their wives. But, then, I remembered that, before a career in mental health, I was trained as a journalist and that I had maintained a weekly opinion column in the Port Harcourt-based Daily Sunray newspaper in which I had addressed every topic of my fancy. At that time, all I needed was to get a set of facts on any topic and use my professional insight to offer an informed comment. That's how I decided to wear my journalism hat, in this exercise, rather than that of a clinician.

As someone who grew up in Igbo land and has lived in the United States for 14 years and after speaking with a number of people in the course of gathering information for this book, I can assert that a feeling of loss may have led the affected Igbo men to kill their wives. To varying degrees, and as mediated by many factors, almost all Igbo men who immigrated to the United State after the age of 18 are dealing with loss – a loss of power, control and authority. For some, this sense of loss approximates a trauma, in its effect on their lives and relationships, particularly with their wives. The good news is that our children, the second and subsequent generations of Igbo people in the United States, may not be beholden by this powerlessness and, therefore, will be less susceptible to domestic violence than their forebears. Our children are getting practical lessons in gender relations that are more amenable to the demands of the American society, the kind that their parents did not get.

Those of us who grew up in Igbo land or even any other part of Nigeria know that the typical Igbo man arrives the shores of the Western world very powerful and pampered, relative to the Igbo woman. It's not just about the patriarchy that is the social order in Igbo land. It's more about the "African big man" syndrome, particularly for the middle class in Nigeria. As a boy, my very first job, upon graduating from the elementary school, was as a houseboy in Aba. So, I had insider knowledge of the lifestyle of the Igbo "Big man." It is something that people like me grew up aspiring to live – sit there, after work, and watch the TV, read the newspapers or go out and play tennis, etc. At any one point, while I worked as a houseboy, there were always three or four of us serving the same family. And before we left Nigeria to seek economic refuge in the West, many of us had attained that status where we did not worry about cooking, cleaning, changing diapers at the middle of the night, feeding the baby, doing grocery shopping, laundry and much more. In the Diaspora, very few Igbo men, irrespective of social status, are afforded the luxury of the "African big man."

To his houseboy or house girl, the middle- and upper-class Igbo man was king, an absolute ruler whose authority was beyond question. To a lesser degree, the Igbo big man also ruled over his wife and his entire household. Once he enters the shores of America, Britain, Canada, or anywhere else in the western hemisphere, he loses that authority. If he attempts to assert control, he may end up in prison or have his record soiled such that employment opportunity in certain fields is closed to him. That sense of loss has spurred many mental health issues for some Igbo men in the Diaspora, particularly depression, that are largely undiagnosed. As a matter of fact, diagnosing depression in men has always been tricky.

And when it comes to the impact of the change in gender relations, it does appear to me that men are shortchanged in a way that is not always recognized or acknowledged. I personally know a number of Igbo men who have taken up new roles, ordinarily meant for women in the traditional gender relations system. I also know many men who have ceded a lot of authority to their wives when it comes to decision making in the household. But very few Igbo women that I know have taken up the things usually reserved for the man at home. Granted our women have gone into the labor force here and are, in many cases, primary breadwinners for their families. But I don't seem to see many of them who would mow the lawns, iron the clothes for everyone, wash the family car, step up there and replace the light bulb and other things that they perceive are in the territory of men. In many cases, Igbo men have had to take care of themselves and every-one else in the family because their wives work. And this intensifies the sense of loss, for many.

And the sense of loss is exacerbated for many of those who marry nurses. Many nurses, by the nature of their job, work long and irregular hours, the impli-cation of which is that they are not available to their husbands as and when they need them. For the many Igbo men who grew up seeing their mothers at home when dad returns, it's a sign that they are losing control of the wife. That sense of loss is made worse if the wife cannot account for how much money was made from the long overtime hours of work because she keeps her separate bank ac-count into which the money goes. I'm not advocating that our men control their wives here in the manner that our fathers controlled their wives but I ask that we understand what this powerlessness may mean to the typical Igbo man. Even, the mere fact that he's not the primary breadwinner for his household can spark off a feeling of lack of control, a feeling of shame or failure in the average Igbo man. Many of us grew up with the idea that it is our responsibility to provide for our family. It is a responsibility that we assume with pride. It defines the Igbo man and his sense of self-worth. Even some of our women latch on to that to expect the man to provide for the family even when the women make more money than their men. Many of us, men and women alike, are stuck in that mentality. Yet, the reality of the labor market here and the cost of living makes it almost impossible for a family to rely on one income. The challenge for many Igbo men has been to adjust successfully to that reality.

The variety of negative emotions that many Igbo men in the Diaspora feel is often masked by widespread belief that it is a mark of weakness for a man to show emotions publicly. The Igbo society created a myth long ago that a man's heart is cold and unfeeling; that it is a sign of weakness for a man to cry or publicly display emotions of any kind. The typical Igbo man is seen as a fixer, particularly in the household. He is seen as the pillar around which the household stands. He's the solution and therefore it's an anomaly for the Igbo man to seek help. The average Igbo man feels he must hide his flaws from others, lest he would be considered weak. He's made to believe that he cannot cede control to his wife. The result of these, for many Igbo men in the Diaspora, has been undiagnosed mental health problems, particularly depression, which often shows up in rage when the bottled up emotions can no longer but explode.

For many Igbo men who were raised to feel superior to women, the whole idea of the equality of the sexes has been difficult to reconcile or accept. And the situation is compounded when their wives happen to earn more money or take advantage of the protections offered by US laws to assert their authority to their incomes or their other freedoms. The resultant feeling of inferiority for the man and his attempt to conjure superiority has spurred all manner of defense mechanisms that create relationship problems for them and their wives.

There is a lot going wrong for the average Igbo man in the Diaspora that can cause emotional distress, which in turn negatively affects the mental health of the Igbo man. Anger, as is displayed by many Igbo men at the slightest perceived provocation can be a symptom of depression and we shouldn't wait until it is transformed into violence, before it is addressed. It's time for Igbo men to use all fora available to them, including the Internet-based electronic groups, to start a discussion on ways to change the cycle of stigma around mental health. It's time to start discussions around the signs and symptoms of depression among men, particularly Igbo men and how they can seek help on time; that it's okay to admit to emotional vulnerability without seeing it as a weakness. We know that, in Igbo land, the stigma surrounding mental illness is so deep that few are willing to address it but, here in the US, we can show that our help seeking behavior reflects that we are no longer in Igbo land; that it is a mark of strength to reach out for help when you need it. At any available opportunities, please, touch that your Igbo man friend, look into his eyes and ask him how he's feeling. Then wait patiently for an answer without any body language that suggests that you'll judge him or spill the beans about his true state of mind, should he open up to you!

www.ingramcontent.com/pod-product-compliance
Lightning Source LLC
Chambersburg PA
CBHW060801050426
42449CB00008B/1478